# THE
# ALCHEMICAL
# SEARCH
## FOR THE
# UNIFIED FIELD

# THE
# ALCHEMICAL
# SEARCH
## FOR THE
# UNIFIED FIELD

Pythagorean, Hermetic, *and*
Shamanic Journeys *into*
Invisible *and* Ethereal Realms

**A Sacred Planet Book**

# R. E. KRETZ

Inner Traditions
Rochester, Vermont

Inner Traditions
One Park Street
Rochester, Vermont 05767
www.InnerTraditions.com

**Sacred Planet Books** are curated by Richard Grossinger, Inner Traditions editorial board member and cofounder and former publisher of North Atlantic Books. The Sacred Planet collection, published under the umbrella of the Inner Traditions family of imprints, includes works on the themes of consciousness, cosmology, alternative medicine, dreams, climate, permaculture, alchemy, shamanic studies, oracles, astrology, crystals, hyperobjects, locutions, and subtle bodies.

Cataloging-in-Publication Data for this title is available from the Library of Congress

ISBN 978-1-64411-782-8 (print)
ISBN 978-1-64411-783-5 (ebook)

Printed and bound in the United States by Versa Press, Inc.

10  9  8  7  6  5  4  3  2  1

Text design and layout by Debbie Glogover
This book was typeset in Garamond Premier Pro with Frontage Condensed, Gill Sans MT Pro and ITC Legacy Sans Std used as display typefaces

To send correspondence to the author of this book, mail a first-class letter to the author c/o Inner Traditions • Bear & Company, One Park Street, Rochester, VT 05767, and we will forward the communication.

*To my wife, Tami, for her love and support.*

*To Charles Kennedy, who showed me the way.*

*For my ancestors, descendants, and those who quest,*
*may this flame illuminate.*

*What we have done for ourselves alone dies with us; what*
*we have done for others and the world remains and is*
*immortal.*

ALBERT PIKE

# CONTENTS

PART 3

# CANDLE

# ACKNOWLEDGMENTS

There are many to whom I owe a debt of gratitude for inspiration, encouragement, assistance, and support. Foremost is my wife, Tami. Her support, sacrifice, proofreading, editing, and good counsel for the past ten years made this endeavor possible. Most of all I thank her for her good humor and tolerance of my being an incessant raconteur of medieval history. A hearty thanks to Dr. Michael and Mary Yannetti for their invaluable friendship, encouragement, guidance, proofreading, and editing as this work came to fruition. A special shout-out and thank-you to Richard Grossinger of Sacred Planet Books who provided the opportunity to have this book published, and to the staff of Inner Traditions • Bear and Company who made it a reality.

# THE BELL, THE BOOK, THE CANDLE

"I am many things, yet I am nothing more than a man"; this is my reply. Some see me as an occult magus, some as a shaman. Some claim that I'm something else still. We are what we are as perceived within the construct of another's reality. That said, I'm fortunate to have had experiences leading to the acquisition of unique knowledge. Some of what I've learned and know has been handed down for generations. Most of what I've learned and know was acquired through a lifetime of personal study and effort. Some knowledge was gifted.

This book is allegorically structured as a quest for the Philosophers' Stone, a quest for the Grail, alchemically mirroring the degrees of Freemasonry and the construct and function of the third eye. In the third part of this book, you'll meet Charles. Charles was the Hermit atop the mountain of knowledge, holding his lantern high for me, the esoteric Fool seeking the flower of wisdom, to follow.

Historical discussion in the first part of the book provides the foundation for the natural philosophy of the Order of Ophiuchus and metempsychosis. It reflects the "Pythagorean" aspect of the book's subtitle, and it's the necessary stabilizing form of the body, a pillar of strength, salt, and corn; it's a square concealing the points of the compasses representing the mind and spirit of the Entered Apprentice degree; it performs as a resistor in an electrical system, as the pituitary gland regulating physiological and psychological processes and emotions. It's the bell.

The alchemical and mechanical aspects of the Stone addressed in the second section of the book, reflecting the "Hermetic" portion of the book's subtitle, equate to a Fellow Craft Mason laboring in the quarry of his mind to craft a perfect ashlar, erecting a pillar of knowledge, exemplified by the revelation of one point of the compasses over the square, symbolizing use of his mind over body, over matter, the union of heaven and earth, or the pineal gland functioning as a capacitor to store and modulate patterns and rhythms or thought. It's the book.

The "shamanic" dimension of the book's subtitle is reflected in the spiritual journey illuminating the third part of the book—that of a Master Mason traveling a rough road. Assailed by ruffians, he aspires to gain the summit of the mountain of knowledge. Having experienced life, death, and rebirth, his is a spiritual quest for the flower of wisdom, the pillar of beauty, symbolized as mercury, the elusive Atalanta, and wine. As a Master Mason, both points of the compasses are now placed atop the square, forming a spiritual arch bridging the pillars of strength and wisdom, body and mind. In the midst of the arch is a keystone, our soul: revealing the invisible ethereal aspects and binding both mind and spirit to the visible, physical, body, much as the thalamus functions as an inductor controlling consciousness and sensory and motor signals that maintains equilibrium—in other words, decision. It's the candle.

Together, the three sections of the book, the three degrees of Masonry, and the three components of the third eye form a veil of First Matter for us to contemplate, a mantra for meditation to become enlightened souls: sulfur, oil, oneness with the universe, and attainment of the Grail. Thus, this book will come full circle: alpha omega alpha (AΩA), an ouroboros, Ophiuchus the serpent bearer. The book is a triangle in its essence, a quadrangle in its quality. It is a *tetractys* devised by Pythagoras and the symbol of a High Priest in Royal Arch Masonry.

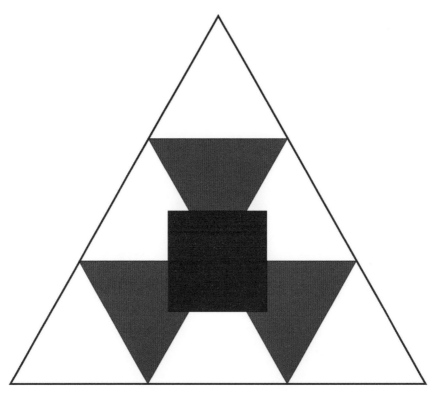

*Figure P.1. Symbol of a Royal Arch Mason High Priest within a tetractys.*

Knowledge comes to each of us from many places and in many ways. When we have eyes to see, ears to hear, and a heart to recognize and appreciate it for what it is; when we are duly and truly prepared to receive it, knowledge comes. You have been gifted a treasure map for the scientific and personal pursuit of the occult, that which is hidden, the divine. Use it wisely! This book *is* the Philosophers' Stone! Ring the bell, open the book, light the candle!

# INTRODUCTION

# MY CURIOSITY FOR TRUTH

This is the first in a series of works on the Order of Ophiuchus. Primarily it discusses what the Philosophers' Stone is and addresses the mechanics of its employment from an alchemical perspective influencing Freemasonry. We then apply what we have learned to a spiritual journey where our vehicle is allegorical lessons imparted by a shaman who is steeped in Native American traditions. In both regards, this effort differentiates itself from other esoteric works in its approach, shedding light on heretofore seldom-revealed occult knowledge.

Many books have been written about the Masons, Templars, and Rosicrucians, mostly by non-Masons. While professionally researched, without the benefit of personally experiencing initiatory degrees and lectures, their works fail to capture the ancient esoteric secrets of the fraternity or its historical essence. As an analogy, it's like a man writing a book about menopause or childbirth. Regardless of how well he's researched those topics, a man cannot fully capture the physical, mental, emotional, or hormonal changes involved because he hasn't personally experienced them. Non-Mason writers tend to emphasize selected bits and pieces of incomplete regurgitated and incorrect institutional history: the Templar downfall, the Grail, or treasure, and so forth. Then too, modern Mason writers on the subject are often only existential in their approach and miss the layered allegorical messages inculcated by the ancient mystery schools. (In saying these writers provide existential answers, I mean that they primarily address the existence and forms of human nature.) When asked directly about the secrets of Freemasonry such writers often obfuscate, as they simply don't know what the "secrets" might be. They are what we refer to in the Craft as speculative Masons. *Speculative* is a polite word for guessing; these writers often presume a moral equivalent for an allegorical unknown.

In contrast to speculative Masons are operative Masons, the performers, the doers. As an operative Mason I've spent many years studying and learning history with an emphasis on how layered symbolic meaning was employed by the ancients to simultaneously communicate encrypted information to different groups contingent on their acquired level of knowledge. This is what differentiates my work from what has been published and promulgated by other so-called authorities.

Going forward, your attitudes, beliefs, and values, as well as the comfort of your worldview paradigm, will be challenged. To comprehend the Craft, Templars, and Rosicrucians it's imperative to not only think outside of the box, but to remove the construct of the box. When seeking the truth one must ask what truth is. "Truth is a battle of perceptions. People only see what they're prepared to confront. It's not what you look at that matters, but what you see. And when different perceptions battle against one another, the truth has a way of getting lost and the monsters find a way of getting out."[1]

First and foremost, allow me to make it clear that the knowledge, perspective, and opinions communicated in this book are those of the author. They have not been approved, sanctioned, encouraged, or supported by any Masonic body, nor should they be construed to be.

Much of the esoteric material covered here is not known even to the most elite Masons. Therefore, Masons you may know just aren't aware of these things. Most aren't interested, nor do they want to know. Why? For several reasons. They're your husbands, brothers, sons, friends, and neighbors. It's socially and religiously unacceptable to want to know about hidden knowledge, admit knowing it, or worse, attempt to discuss it. To do so incurs an unnecessary risk of being ostracized and labeled. No, it's better to remain within our comfort zone of socially and religiously acceptable attitudes, beliefs, and values. An open, knowledge-seeking mind that thinks freely threatens comfort. It's the mark of a heretic! Better to maintain the status quo; better to remain ignorant. Ignorance is bliss! So, asking a Mason about these mysteries is pointless. They just don't know and are for the most part clueless. It's not to say that some won't attempt to baffle you with bullshit, dazzle you with tap-dancing nonsense, or divert your attention and change the subject in an effort to diffuse your questions and avoid admitting their ignorance. This does and will happen!

I was initiated as a Mason in 2003, while in my late forties. My father was a Mason, as was his father and grandfathers for generations on both sides. My family's Masonic connections included friendship with founding fathers such as General Washington and Thomas Jefferson. They had a close relationship with Napoleon. An uncle, Matthew Sutcliffe, a colleague and New World venture partner of John Dee and Sir Francis Bacon, financed the voyages of Captain John Smith of Pocahontas fame, was chaplain to both Queen Elizabeth I and King James VI and I, and founder of Chelsea College. Johan Valentin Andreae, an alleged founder of modern Rosicrucianism, attended Tübingen University where he received instruction from my relatives who established it. These same relatives, the Cottas, published Andreae's, Schiller's, and Goethe's books and housed Martin Luther, a Rosicrucian affiliate and father of the Protestant Reformation, while he attended Georgenschule in Eisenach from 1498 to 1501.

Masonry and Rosicrucianism are an integral part of my heritage. By becoming a Mason, I was perpetuating my family's centuries-old tradition, and it became an important part of my life. In time, with hard work, I became Master of a Lodge, High Priest of a Royal Arch Chapter, Illustrious Master of a Council of Cryptic Masons, Commander of a Commandery of Knights Templar, and District Deputy Grand Commander of Knights Templar. I served as Grand Sentinel of a Grand Commandery of Knights Templar and earned the Knight York

Cross of Honor (KYCH) and the 32nd degree in the Scottish Rite (SJ). I was invited into appendant Masonic bodies such as Knights Masons, the York Rite Sovereign College, Order of the Red Cross of Constantine, Order of St. Thomas, the Royal Order of Scotland, and perhaps the most prestigious body, the Societas Rosicruciana in Civitatibus Foederatis (SRICF), that is, the Rosicrucians, which, in the United States, is limited to 72 Masons per state out of an average of 35,000 Master Masons.

One could say I know a thing or two about a thing or two that you're naturally curious about but don't really want to know. You really don't want to know because you may learn something that conflicts with what you *think* you know: something that may make you uncomfortable; something you can't reconcile with what you've been taught or your entrenched attitudes, beliefs, and values; something that you may subsequently find offensive—*the truth*. And yet, here you are, reading this book. If it's any comfort, I can tell you this much: *God is real.* The Bible, the Qur'an, the Vedas, and many other ancient texts and stories relate the truth—just not in the way you have been taught or think or believe.

After I was raised as a Master Mason I had questions that my esteemed brothers with many years of membership and experience couldn't answer. I wanted to know the meanings of symbols and other things, such as the cable tow, that they couldn't reasonably explain away with their existentialist answers. I was told that I asked too many questions and should focus on learning ritual. Ritual work—verbatim rote regurgitation and reenactment of what occurs in the Masonic degrees and lectures—was all that mattered. I was repeatedly told that everything I needed to know was contained in the ritual. What about the "secrets of Freemasonry" that I was promised would be revealed? It's in the ritual. What are the symbolic meanings of the ritual? It's in the ritual. After unsatisfactory existentialist, biblical, and moral explanations, I was continually admonished to learn the ritual. The answers are in the ritual. You ask too many questions. Essentially I was admonished to "pay no attention to the man behind the curtain."

For many years I felt that Masonic rituals, catechisms, and lectures were incongruent, but as these things are the heart of Masonry's sacred teachings, who was I to dare question them? Doing so would be much more than disrespecting my esteemed brethren, it would be perceived as trammeling upon the Craft and violating my obligations. That I would not do! Yet, questions persistently arose, gnawing at me.

I was compelled to saddle up and search for light, to search for knowledge on my own with little more than the hope that I wouldn't be jousting with windmills in a quixotic quest. I began reading voraciously and researching, hoping to discover hidden meanings, hidden truths, "secrets." As I mentioned previously, many Masonic writings provide only existential answers. Masonry, on the other hand, is multifaceted, embracing and encompassing much more than human nature. Masonry attempts to address physical nature—all that is tangible and perceptible around us. Masonry also attempts to address abstract concepts beyond the physical, such as our spirit and our soul. Masonry is a quest not only for universal truths, but our place and purpose within the universe— who we are and where we come from.

What is the truth that Masons seek? Does truth equate to enlightenment? Perhaps truth, or enlightenment, is understanding not only ourselves but how everything in the universe is integrated, interdependent, and strives to achieve balance: unity, peace, and harmony. Such was the perspective of ancient cultures. They observed the relationships and interactions of all they could see and hear—terrestrial and celestial, movable and immovable—noting patterns and rhythmic cycles culminating in birth, life, death, and regeneration. Esoteric ancients captured and communicated these patterns and cycles mouth-to-ear, in allegorical ritual reenactment, allusion, illusion, and symbolism. As such, these things, these "secrets," have been passed on to us. Today Masons still communicate these secrets mouth-to-ear, perform allegorical rituals, and display symbols. Unfortunately, most don't "see" or "hear" that which is hidden in its degrees. To "see" and "hear" as our ancient predecessors did requires a major paradigm shift in our worldview.

The "truths" I sought remained elusive for some time. It has been a challenging and lonely journey along a treacherously narrow path—a path where I have been beset by ruffians and many incidents have occurred. Often, I wanted to give up, to quit and have nothing more to do with it. But somehow, somehow, I found the strength and courage to continue. I found a set of keys! It was a set of keys that unlocked doors to discovering hidden answers. These keys were there all along, hidden in plain sight. I just didn't recognize them for what they were. I was first made a Mason in my heart, but I wasn't duly and truly prepared. When I was ready to receive it, when I remembered in whom to place my trust, then knowledge—light—was revealed.

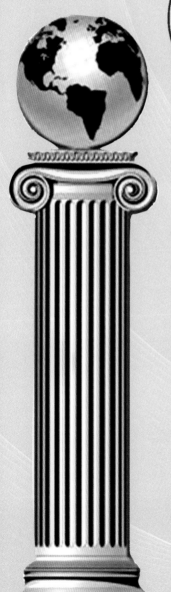

# PART 1

# BELL

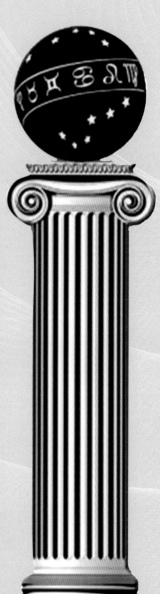

# 1
# THE ORDER OF OPHIUCHUS

## WHAT IS THE ORDER OF OPHIUCHUS?

The Order of Ophiuchus is a system of natural, personal philosophy that uses a Pythagorean approach to address metempsychosis. Inspired by natural philosophers of the past, the Order of Ophiuchus considers that God exists and that he gave us the ability to reason in accordance with the theory of knowledge in order to form justified beliefs. Therefore, in accordance with ideas and concepts found in Rosicrucianism, Freemasonry, Martinism, Theosophy, Hermeticism, and so forth, the Order of Ophiuchus is a personal, wide-ranging quest for truth using the seven liberal arts and seven universal principles as its platform. In this regard, "order" alludes to the arrangement or disposition of things in relation to each other according to a particular sequence, pattern, or method. It is an attempt to discern the process cycle of Divine Love in accordance with the Pythagorean idea that all things are composed of numbers and that the principles of mathematics are the principles of all things, binding the terrestrial realm of Earth to the celestial kingdom of Heaven. Its foundation was in ancient Greece and was influenced by Egyptian and Mesopotamian cultures.

## THE SYMBOL OF
## THE ORDER OF OPHIUCHUS

In this personal philosophy, the symbol of the Order of Ophiuchus is a green ouroboros encircling a red cross of Saint George. Overlaying the center of the cross is a white downward triangle over a black upward triangle. There is a dot, or point, in the center.

The green ouroboros denotes the duality of the regenerative cycle of nature: AΩA. The ouroboros is overlaid on and encircles a red cross of St. George, creating a solar cross, indicating we are ruled by the Sun. The arms of the cross represent the four elements (fire, water, air, and earth) and the four cardinal directions (north, east, south, and west). They also represent time as the solstices and equinoxes and as the four seasons. Overlaying the crux in the center of the circle is a white downward triangle symbolizing the purity of knowledge of the sacred feminine overlaying a black upward triangle indicating the strength of

*Figure 1.1. The symbol of the Order of Ophiuchus.*

hidden wisdom acquired through experience and the fall of man. The merged white and black triangles also denote the union of opposites, male and female, black and white, life and death, wisdom and knowledge. Within the white triangle, centered on the crux, is a point that binds all of the elements together. As a whole, the point within the circle of the symbol represents the soul of man within the spirit of the universe as we know it, the microcosm within the macrocosm.

The motto of the order is γνῶθι σεαυτόν (*gnōthi seauton*), which means "know thyself" in Greek. In Latin the phrase is *nosce te ipsum*. It is the first of three maxims inscribed on the forecourt of the Temple of Apollo at Delphi. The other two maxims are "nothing to excess" and "certainty brings insanity."

## WHO IS OPHIUCHUS?

Ophiuchus was considered a great healer and was associated with Asclepius, a son of Apollo. According to mythology, Asclepius was taught the art of medicine by Chiron the centaur. One day Asclepius saw a snake resurrect another snake by laying herbs on it. He began using those herbs and not only healed the sick but managed to raise the dead. In another story, Asclepius was given the power to resurrect the dead, including Orion, by the goddess Athena. That Asclepius learned the secret of immortality upset Hades, the god of the underworld. Hades complained to Zeus that the flow of souls to the underworld would cease because of what Asclepius was doing. Zeus agreed, killing Asclepius with a lightning bolt, then placing him among the stars as the constellation Ophiuchus, which means "serpent bearer" in Greek. The constellation Ophiuchus is sometimes depicted as Apollo wrestling the serpent Python.

The constellation Ophiuchus straddles the celestial equator opposite the asterism of Orion. Technically Ophiuchus doesn't belong to the zodiac family of constellations, but rather to the Hercules family of constellations. There are only twelve zodiacal signs in Western sidereal astrology. However, some incorporate Ophiuchus as a thirteenth sign between Scorpio and Sagittarius, spanning the days from approximately November 29 to December 17 based on the first-century CE astronomical poem, *Astronomica,* by Marcus Manilius. Inclusion of Ophiuchus as a thirteenth sign makes sense if we consider the zodiac as twelve plus one and that Ophiuchus is neither ruled by a planet nor associated with an element. As such, it suggests that Ophiuchus is separate and superior, ruling or overseeing the zodiacal signs in a twelve-plus-one capacity. Rooted in antiquity, there are many examples of twelve plus one, for example, Abraham and his twelve sons, Jesus and his twelve apostles, Hercules and his twelve labors, Arthur and his twelve knights, a judge and twelve jurors, and so forth. Keep in mind that twelve plus one is also an anagram for eleven plus two in that both phrases use the same thirteen letters.

In October 1604 Johannes Kepler observed and documented a new star in the ankle of Ophiuchus. Known as Kepler's Supernova (SN-1604), it was visible from October 1604 through April 1606. At one point it was seen during the day for a period of three weeks. Astrologers of the time, including John Dee, considered it as fulfillment of the prophecy of Paracelsus and that the astronomical events of 1603 to 1604 were signs and harbingers of approaching revolution: "there is nothing concealed which will not be revealed."

Fludd stated that the 1604 celestial events were a sign for the Rosicrucians to emerge from their period of secrecy to expand their membership and begin restoration of the world. It's at this time that we find Freemasonry beginning to emerge in London, spreading to Germany, France, Italy, and the New World.

But these societies did not emerge from thin air. Their histories go back to ancient Greece.

## THE APOLLO-PARNASSUS CONNECTION

Many ancient mystery schools, certainly Rosicrucianism and Freemasonry, are rooted in myth and legend involving Mount Parnassus in ancient Greece. It is there, on Mount Parnassus, that we find ties of the celestial realm to our terrestrial world. Mount Parnassus effectively means the "mountain of the house of the god," referring to Apollo, the sun god. Its snowcapped twin peaks can appear as a double *A*. Some may esoterically interpret these twin peaks as representing Apollo and his twin sister, Artemis—for whom Diana is the Roman equivalent— and therefore as symbolic of duality. In Ovid's *Metamorphoses,* Mount Parnassus is where Deucalion's ark came to rest in the Greek flood myth. Corycian Cave, located on the slopes of Mount Parnassus, was sacred to Pan, whose homeland was rustic Arcadia.

Located high on the slopes of Mount Parnassus, where a sacred spring emanates from a vaporous cavern, is the Oracle of Delphi. To the ancient Greeks, Delphi was the navel (omphalos), the center of the world. In the Pythagorean parlance of Philolaus of Croton, the navel was the seat of implantation and growth of the embryo from which future growth and nutrition was provided—much like a beehive. In ancient times a beehive-shaped omphalos stone was kept in the inner sanctum of the temple (fig. 1.2, p. 14). It was supported by a bronze tripod, possibly held by three dancers atop a column. Pausanias suggests that it had two gilded eagles on top of it and that it was protected by a woolen cloth with precious stones in the form of a mermaid. It's said that in an attempt to locate the center of the Earth, Zeus launched two eagles from opposite ends of the Earth. From where their paths crossed Zeus threw a stone that landed at Delphi, marking the navel of the world.

According to Greek mythology the site at Delphi originally belonged to Gaia. Gaia was the Greek equivalent of the Sumerian goddess Ninhursag, a primordial deity who was the ancestral mother of all life and primal Earth goddess. As such, she was also a chthonic deity to whom black lambs were sacrificed. Gaia is often depicted as a reclining matronly woman holding a baby or else surrounded by infant gods who were the fruits of the Earth. The cave of the oracle symbolized the womb of the Earth and was guarded by Gaia's giant serpent-dragon child named Python. Apollo usurped Gaia's chthonic powers

*Figure 1.2. The omphalos at Delphi dates to ca. 1400 BCE.*
*This Roman copy is housed at the Archaeological Museum of Delphi.*
*Photo by Zde.*

*Figure 1.3. An engraving of Apollo killing Python by Virgil Solis for Ovid's Metamorphoses, book 1 (1581) (left), is reminiscent of the 1508 woodcut of Saint George slaying the dragon by Wolf Traut (right).*

by killing Python with his arrows, similar to the later story of Saint George slaying the dragon. He took possession of her oracle and built his temple over Gaia's at Delphi. Afterward Apollo's priestess assumed the oracle's prophetic powers and acquired the name Pythia in honor of slain Python. Another myth suggests that Apollo expelled Gaia's twin guardian serpents and wrapped their bodies around Hermes's winged staff known as the caduceus.

The earliest evidence of an oracle at Delphi can be traced to about 1600 BCE. Apollo's priests from Delos, associated with the rise of importance of the city of Corinth, took over the Doric shrine in about the eighth century BCE, but retained the priestess as the oracle dedicated to Gaia to keep the peace. According to tradition, the first Pythia of the Apollo period was Phemonoe, a poet and alleged daughter of Apollo. Initially priestesses were young virgins from Delphi, but after Echecrates of Thessaly kidnapped and violated a young and beautiful Pythia in the late third century BCE, a woman older than fifty was chosen for the position.

Priestesses of Delphi ceased all family responsibilities, marital relations, and forfeited their individual identity. Three priestesses usually served as the Pythia, two taking turns giving prophecies with another in reserve. Prophecies were only given during the nine warmest months of the year, and then during only one day of the month, on the seventh, after a ritual purification rite.

At the top of the pediment of the Temple of Apollo (god of light and solar worship) is the letter Epsilon. For many reasons, the placement of this letter on the temple is thought to be related to Delphic solar mysticism. It connects Apollo with light, divinity, man, and self-knowledge.

> Its placement . . . indicates the man's eternal relationship with the light, thus, perfection. The letter E has three parallel lines marking the union of body, mind, and soul, highlighting the trinity of human nature. The letter is the fifth number of the Greek alphabet, with the number five symbolizing the five elements needed for life, according to the Ancients: Earth, Air, Water, Fire and Aether.

The Delphic Epsilon was placed at the top of the pediment of the Temple of Apollo, right at its center. At the lower-left corner, there was the inscription "Γνῶθι Σαυτόν," meaning "know thyself" in Greek, while at the lower-right corner, there was the inscription "Μηδέν Ἄγαν," meaning "nothing in excess." These are known as the "Delphic Commandments" and E was "presiding" over them.[1]

## THE APOLLO-PARNASSUS-PYTHAGORAS CONNECTION

The name Pythagoras (570–495 BCE) combines *pythios,* denoting the cult of Apollo at Delphi, with *agora,* meaning "assembly." Roughly, the name translates as "Apollo's assembly" or "society of Apollo" and may or may not have been his actual birth name. Pythagoras and his followers thought of themselves as a fraternity of Apollo, a brotherhood dedicated to the sun, referring to knowledge as light and illumination as the foundation of ancient mystery schools, which would come to include the original Knights Templar.

In the sixteenth century what remained of the moribund Knights Templar was remodeled and revitalized by John Dee and Sir Francis Bacon. They merged the Templar's Pythagorean and Rosicrucian concepts and practices with the Freemason's operative-guild structure to create a society known as the Honorable Knights of the Helmet. While the helmet referred to the Cap of Invisibility, also known as the Helm of Hades, worn by the goddess Pallas Athena during the Trojan War, the society was dedicated to her brother Apollo. Sir Francis Bacon, as the titular head of the Knights of the Helmet, a.k.a. the "invisibles," was known as Apollo. It's important to note that the guilds of the Freemasons evolved separately from the Knights Templar to become, like the Templar's chaplains, a *category* of Templar. Not all Masons were affiliated with the Knights Templar, nor were all Templars affiliated with the Freemasons.

It's claimed that Pythagoras traveled and studied extensively abroad. The Egyptians are said to have taught him geometry, the Phoenicians arithmetic, the Chaldeans astronomy, and the Magi the principles of religion and practical maxims for the conduct of life. According to Diogenes Laërtius, Pythagoras not only visited Egypt and learned the Egyptian language (as reported by Antiphon in his *On Men of Outstanding Merit*), but he also "journeyed among the Chaldeans and Magi." Later in Crete, he went to the Cave of Ida with Epimenides, and also traveled to and entered Egyptian sanctuaries for the purpose of learning information concerning the secret lore of the different gods. The Middle Platonist biographer Plutarch (ca. 46–120 CE) writes in his treatise *On Isis and Osiris* that, during his visit to Egypt, Pythagoras received instruction from the Egyptian priest Oenuphis of Heliopolis. Other ancient writers also mention Pythagoras's visit to Egypt. According to the Christian theologian Clement of Alexandria (ca. 150–215 CE), "Pythagoras was a disciple of Soches, an Egyptian arch prophet, as well as Plato of Sechnuphis of Heliopolis."[2]

Pythagoras was legendary even in his own time. He was said to dress all in white and wear a golden wreath upon his head in the style of

Apollo. According to Aristotle, he showed Abaris the Hyperborean his golden thigh, proving that he was the Hyperborean Apollo. Aristotle also claimed in a fragment that when a poisonous snake bit Pythagoras, he bit it back, killing it. Allegedly a priest of Apollo gifted Pythagoras a magic arrow that enabled him to fly over long distances and perform ritual purifications. Later, Roman legend claimed that Pythagoras was the son of Apollo and, according to Muslim tradition, he was initiated as a mystic by Hermes, the messenger of the gods, who was also a shepherd god, a chthonic god, a god of boundaries, and a protector of orators, merchants, travelers, and thieves.

In about 530 BCE Pythagoras established a school in Croton along the coast of southern Italy. Initiates were sworn to secrecy and practiced a communal ascetic lifestyle resembling that of later Christian monasteries, as well as a form of vegetarianism. Pythagoras is credited with many philosophical, scientific, and mathematical ideas, including:

- The concept of metempsychosis, or the transmigration of the soul, that suggests that every soul is immortal and, upon death, enters a new body. In broad terms Pythagoras addresses the ideas of rebirth and regeneration. However, his idea goes well beyond that and speaks to the laws of thermodynamics developed in the 1850s, more than two thousand years later. The first law of thermodynamics, known as the law of conservation of energy, states that energy can neither be created nor destroyed—only converted from one form of energy to another. In other words, energy cannot be made from nothing. The second law of thermodynamics, known as the law of entropy, says that energy disperses creating chaos. For chaos to perpetuate, order is required. Nature creates pockets of order through life. Life disperses energy; the more life, the better energy is dispersed. Life obeys and exists because of the law of entropy.
- The notion of sphericity of the Earth; that the Earth was roughly round, a sphere.

- The division of the Earth into five climatic zones: one torrid, two temperate, and two frigid, and that the central torrid zone was uninhabitable because of the heat from the direct rays of the sun.
- The determination that that the "morning" and "evening" stars were the planet Venus rising and setting.
- The foundation of numerology, believing all things are composed of numbers; that the principles of mathematics were the principles of all things; that odd numbers were masculine and even numbers were feminine; and that numbers related to intangible concepts.
  - The number 1, not always considered a number, was the monad. It was a noble number, the number of reason and wisdom, representing the origin of all things as both male and female; found in heaven as the divine masculine.
  - The number 2 was the dyad (duad), representing duality, matter, and ignorance. It was the first even or female number, the number of opinion, signifying the sacred feminine, "the deep," and water in opposition to the monad.
  - The number 3, the triad, the first true male number, refers to knowledge, equilibrium, and is the number of harmony. Because it had a beginning, middle, and end, he believed that the number three was the sum of the world and all things in it. It signified the mind, was considered the "ideal" number, and revered as a symbol of Apollo. The triad represents the three primary colors and major heavenly bodies (sun, moon, and stars).
  - The number 4, the tetrad, was the number of justice or retribution. It signified the four elements, the four seasons, balance, and the body. It was the primogenial number, the root of all things, the fountain of nature, symbolic of God, the soul of man, and the most perfect number. The tetrad represents the four secondary colors and minor heavenly bodies.
  - The number 5, the pentad, sometimes referred to as the Hierophant or Priest of Mysteries, represented marriage, as it was the sum of the numbers two and three. It also symbolized

nature and the substance of vitality and life known as "the ether" that permeated the other four elements, signifying conquest of our spiritual nature over our material nature, mind over matter. Symbolically it's represented as a five-pointed star or Hugieia Pentagram.

- The number 6, the hexad, was the number of creation of the world, harmony, and the soul. It's the union of two triangles that are opposites.

- The number 7, the heptad, was sacred because Apollo's birthday was celebrated on the seventh of the month. It represented the number of heavenly bodies viewed from Earth, and the number of strings on Apollo's lyre. It is the number of the law and the number of religion and worthy of veneration.

- The number 8, the ogdoad, was considered the holy number. It is the number of the first cube, formed in part by the twisted snakes of Hermes's caduceus.

- The number 9, the ennead, is the first square of an odd number (3 × 3). A limitless number, it is the number of man because it represents man's nine months of gestation that falls short of perfection by one. It was also perceived as an evil number as it was an inverted "6," brought forth by the union of opposites that formed it.

- The number 10, the decad, was the perfect number, exemplified by the tetractys made up of of ten equilateral triangles. It was the number of the universe, heaven, and the world.

• The consideration that one point was the generator of dimensions; two points were the generator of a line of one dimension; three points were the generator of a triangle of two dimensions; and that four points were the generator of a tetrahedron of three dimensions.

• The theory of proportions: that number gives rise to *proportion* and *proportion* gives rise to harmony. The universe is sustained by harmony and therefore music. Music purified the soul, and different types of music were used to either calm or arouse the soul.

- The system of Pythagorean tuning, in which the frequency ratios of all intervals are based on the ratio 3:2. Known as the "pure" perfect fifth, it is one of the easiest to tune by ear.

- The suggestion of *musica universalis,* or harmony of the spheres, that proposes the planets and stars move according to mathematical equations and resonate to produce an inaudible symphony of music (fig. 1.4, p. 22). Music (sound) and color (light) are vibrations at frequencies within ranges that we use our senses to hear, see, and feel. The seven observable bodies in our solar system equate to the seven musical notes and visible-light-spectrum colors. Musical chords are any harmonic set of pitches/frequencies consisting of multiple notes that are heard as if sounding simultaneously. A basic chord consists of three notes, a triad, consisting of a root, a major or minor third, and a perfect fifth. This correlates with the structure of our solar system that has seven observable bodies from Earth (Sun, Moon, Mercury, Venus, Mars, Jupiter, and Saturn), five planets beyond Earth (Mars, Jupiter, Saturn, Uranus, and Neptune), and the three inner planets closest to the Sun (Mercury, Venus, and Earth). For example, the chord of C major uses C (the Sun) as its root note, E (Mercury) as its major third, and G (Mars) as its perfect fifth. Therefore, C major combines the three primary colors or red, yellow, and blue to produce white.

- The Pythagorean theorem, also known as the 47th problem of Euclid, fundamental to Euclidean geometry (fig. 1.5, p. 22). What the theorem says is that when a triangle has a right angle (90°) and squares are made of each of the three sides, then the biggest square has the exact same area as the other two squares combined. As a mathematical equation it's written as $a^2 + b^2 = c^2$. This is useful when you know the lengths of two sides of a right triangle and need to determine the length of the third side.

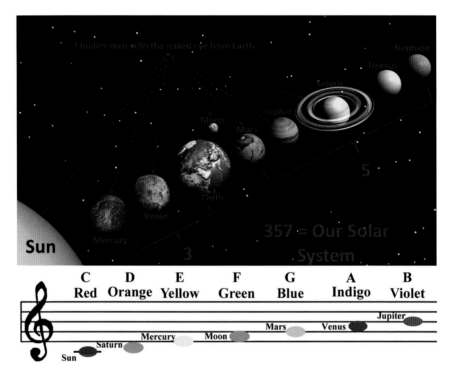

*Figure 1.4. Musica universalis; the harmony of spheres, which utilizes the numbers 3, 5, and 7 in its theory.*

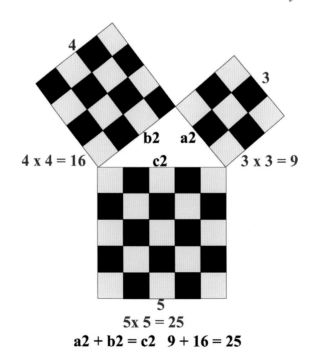

*Figure 1.5. The Pythagorean Theorem, a.k.a. the 47th problem of Euclid, showing a right triangle whose sides are in the ratio of 3:4:5.*

- The five regular or Platonic solids. These are five geometric solids whose faces are all identical, regular polygons meeting at the same three-dimensional angles. They consist of the tetrahedron (or pyramid), cube, octahedron, dodecahedron, and icosahedron.

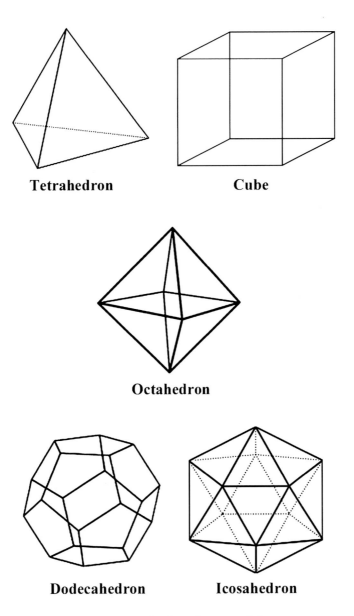

**Tetrahedron**　　　　**Cube**

**Octahedron**

**Dodecahedron**　　　**Icosahedron**

*Figure 1.6. The five Platonic solids.*

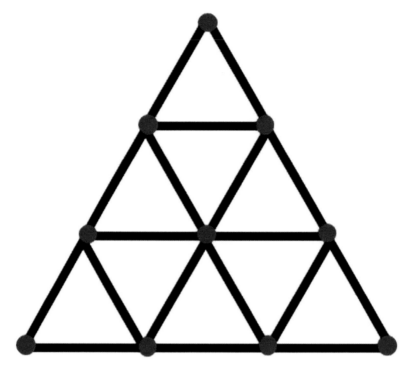

*Figure 1.7. The tetractys.*

- The design of the tetractys, an equilateral triangular form consisting of ten points in four rows. It symbolizes the geometric, arithmetic, and musical ratios that are the foundation upon which the entire universe is built. The tetractys incorporates the symbolism of both the triangle and the number ten. In seed-like form it embraces the principles of the natural world, harmony of the cosmos, and ascent to the divine. It was a symbol of utmost mystical importance that Pythagoreans swore an oath of silence upon.

- The Pythagorean pentacle, an important but often misunderstood symbol used by the Druids, Rosicrucians, Templars, and Masons. The Pythagorean pentacle was a symbol of protection that probably originated in Egypt or Babylon. It was referred to by Pythagoras and his followers as Hugieia (Ugieia), roughly translated as "divine blessing." It was an upright pentacle often circumscribed by a pentagon with the Greek letters *Υ, I, Γ, Θ, A* located at its points. The Pythagorean pentacle served as an alchemical calculator containing the elements, ages of man, organic cycle, planets, tetractys, colors, directions, the four functions and the self, duality, and the alchemical great work that pertains to the Philosophers' Stone and transmigration of the soul. It wasn't until the introduction of Roman Christianity that the pentacle acquired a negative connotation and the erroneous idea of representing magic and witchcraft, and therefore the "Devil."

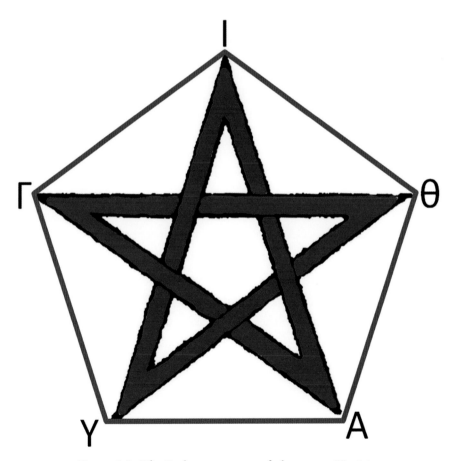

*Figure 1.8. The Pythagorean pentacle known as Hugieia.*

The chart below offers an idea of how the Hugieia functioned as a calculator.

| Letter | Greek Name | Element | Quality | Age | Season | Moon |
|--------|-----------|---------|---------|-----|--------|------|
| HU | Hudor | Water | Cold | Old Age | Winter | 4th Q |
| G | Gaia | Earth | Dry | Maturity | Autumn | 3rd Q |
| I | Iota | Spirit | Divine | Death | Terror | New Moon |
| EI | Heile | Fire | Hot | Youth | Summer | 2nd Q |
| A | Aer | Air | Wet | Child | Spring | 1st Q |

| Letter | Planet | Function | Alchemy | Colors | Sun | Direction |
|--------|--------|----------|---------|--------|-----|-----------|
| HU | Saturn | Sensation | Nigredo | Black/Blue | Night | North |
| G | Mars | Thinking | Rubedo | Red | Evening | West |
| I | Mercury | Self | Iosis | Purple | | Up |
| EI | Jupiter | Intuition | Citrinatis | Yellow | Meridian | South |
| A | Venus | Feeling | Albedo | White/Green | Morning | East |

Pythagoras used the idea that the principles of math are what bind the terrestrial to the celestial to develop his concepts and formulas and thus his understanding of the world. He firmly believed that God gave man the right to reason and, by extension, to know himself and the universe. The Rosicrucians, Templars, and Freemasons would continue his lines of reasoning into their own time—and beyond. In part 2, we will use Pythagoras's ideas to study the Philosophers' Stone. But first, I recommend pausing to ready your mind for that journey.

# 2
# THOUGHTFUL MORSELS

Alchemy, Hermetics, sacred geometry, Kabbalah, gematria, astrology, and other occult arts and sciences all allude to the Stone in their own vague way. Left to speculation, it's difficult to empirically describe what the Stone really is. A quest for the Philosophers' Stone is a quest for the Grail, a search for truth. What we seek is elusive because, first, it appears as an intangible idea, and second, because it appears to be an intangible idea, we have difficulty visualizing it and may not recognize it for what it is. To recognize the Stone, we must have "eyes that see, ears that hear, and hearts that understand." This is to say, we must shift our paradigms and seek it with an open mind without constraint or construct. We must use what knowledge we have of the Stone as an intangible idea to develop a tangible model. The following two chapters will help you prepare to do so. What follows are thoughts for consideration going forward.

## WHAT IS THE SPEED OF THOUGHT?

If the speed of light is 186,282 miles per second in a vacuum, what then is the speed of thought? Speed is measured as distance over time. But does distance apply to thought? If distance as a variable is not applicable to thought, then our formula for calculating its speed will not work. Perhaps thought is pure energy and its speed is calculated as the speed of light squared multiplied by its mass. Does thought have mass?

It has been suggested that the universe is a thought-generated hologram and that all other energies are harmonic manifestations of it. If the universe were indeed a thought-generated hologram and all energies harmonic manifestations of it, is it to suggest past, present, and future thoughts are concurrent, existing simultaneously? Past, present, and future are elements of time, a man-made construct, so how and why are these elements of time differentiated in a hologram? Is time parsed as a sequential part of a process reconciled as harmonic vibratory manifestations akin to the visible-light spectrum? Can we use time as a variable to calculate the speed of thought? Is the speed of thought constrained by distance and time? Or is the speed of thought instantaneous, or at least beyond our present ability to measure it?

When is a thought formed, conceived? Are thoughts conceived in a vacuum or are they conceived in conjunction with—and are they influenced by—other thoughts or knowledge? Is inception or conception of thought identifiable, measurable, quantifiable? Is thought an emanation of light, photons? Does an increase in photon emissions equate to enlightenment?

## THE FALL OF MAN

Man is his own worst enemy, reflected not in a mirror, but by his shadow that follows him everywhere; stalking him, haunting him, reminding him constantly of what he fears most—himself.

## KNOWLEDGE

Knowledge comes to each of us from many places and in many ways. When we have eyes to see, ears to hear, and a heart to recognize and appreciate it for what it is, when we are duly and truly prepared to receive it, knowledge comes.

## ALLEGORY

Language is important because it enables us to communicate as well as to convey knowledge, ideas, and abstract concepts. Linguistic history is the magical marriage of word and meaning, sounds and embodiments, that intonate storied treasures of color through grammar, rhetoric, and logic, fundamental to allegory.

## THE FOOL AND THE HERMIT

*Occult* means that which is hidden or closed-off from view.

*Esoteric* means arcane, mysterious, or secret and intended for, or likely understood by, only a few people with specialized knowledge or interest.

Study of the occult by the esoteric is a journey, not a destination. It's a treacherously narrow path few travel, one illuminated by nothing more than the pale glow of our heart's hope. We begin as Fools, as quixotic knights-errant in need of psychological space, having withdrawn from society, retreating to chambers of reflection. We become meditative and contemplative, absorbed in self-examination and reassessment, unaware of the inherent dangers of windmills, inner-space explorations, and we are oblivious to warnings. Thus along the way, ruffians are encountered, and incidents occur. We must remember in whom we place our trust!

As we quest, we suffer. We experience pain and acquire knowledge. We grow! Applied knowledge improves with lessons learned through experience as it rises in quality, budding and blossoming as wisdom, strength, and beauty, much like Aaron's rod. We have become better than we once were! We have changed and transformed, evolving as a Hermit, as a spiritual advisor, a wise person, a teacher, a mentor. Aged and cloaked in humility and wisdom acquired by many years of

*Figure 2.1. The Fool and the Hermit tarot cards*
*from the Rider-Waite-Smith deck, first published in 1909.*

experience, the Hermit holds his lantern of knowledge high on the mountain, illuminating the occult path, that esoteric Fools may follow his light in his quest for the flower of wisdom.

# 3
# THE KINGDOM OF HEAVEN

What is the Kingdom of Heaven? Is it a theocracy? No, though some may liken it to one. Could it be a metaphor for enlightenment, something experienced when we die or in our living mind when we go to a "better place," an ethereal place of light, of knowledge, where we become one with the universe, the ALL? Could the Kingdom of Heaven be an allegory of the Philosophers' Stone? Let's explore this last idea.

## A UNIVERSAL CYCLE

What does it mean to exist? Is there a difference between existing in the world and existing in the mind? What are the connections between thoughts, words, and things? These were philosophical questions posed by Parmenides. Philo claimed the Scriptures should not be read literally, but as containing hidden truths waiting to be found by those with the patience and will to discover them.

*It is autumn. Seasonal change is in the crisp cool air. It rained last night; all is wet. Looking out my window I see shallow pools of wind-rippled water along our leaf-strewn dirt drive. Wispy mists of early morning fog are rising up from the river and valleys. Leaves on the trees are turning color, gently dropping off. Our hay has been cut and stored away. Birds are flying south for the winter. Deer in rut are breeding in the field below the house. Within the month our landscape will be stark, brown, appearing devoid of its once lush beauty. But it isn't dead; it's resting, dormant, sleeping, soon to be blanketed with snow. Spring will arrive again in a few months; new leaves on the trees and colorful blooms will burst forth; grass will begin to green and grow; birds will fly north to their breeding grounds; and fawns will play in the field below the house. Our landscape will be fresh, verdant, and full of life again, as the world is resurrected. We see birth, growth, maturation, reproduction, death, and regeneration exemplified seasonally. This is nature's cycle. It is a universal cycle.*

## A GLASS OF WATER

Since ancient times man has wrestled with questions of God, creation, nature, and the how and why things are the way they are. One of the earliest Greek philosophers was Thales of Miletus. He argued that water—as it could be vapor, liquid, or solid—was the first principle of life. He also claimed that God was in all things and that the mind of the world is God.

Heraclitus preached duality and that everything is in a universal state of flux between opposites, suggesting both change and motion are both possible and necessary states of nature, that space is a relationship between physical objects. His atomic theory supports Einstein's general theory of relativity in that "Energy cannot be created or destroyed, it can only be changed from one form to another."

*Take a glass of water and drop it! What happens? The glass vessel may or may not break. If it breaks we cleanup the broken pieces and dispose of them. But what actually happens to that glass? In simple terms, it's redistributed, repurposed, reused. If the glass doesn't break we pick it up, clean it, reuse it. At some point in time that glass is destined to break.*

*What has happened to the water in that glass? Does it just go away? No! Some is absorbed in the rag used to sop up the water, then is wrung out in the sink. From the sink it flows to a sewer to be processed and cleaned to fill another glass for us to drink, maybe it finds its way to a stream, river, or an ocean; perhaps your pet drinks some of it; by chance some of it is absorbed by a carpet or wood floor or absorbed into the ground where it nourishes plants and animals. Eventually it will evaporate into the atmosphere creating fog, rain, or snow. The water that is consumed and used today is the same water that has probably always been on this planet. Like everything else, it's repeatedly repurposed, redistributed, reused.*

Pythagoras, in addition to his work in mathematics and music, believed in reincarnation and the transmigration of souls. Our bodies and minds are like a glass, we are a vessel that contains water that is our spirit. We may appear to no longer function and to "die" at some point, but we are really only changing form to be reused. Water represents, and contains, our life force, our spirit. Water is part of everything that lives, and everything that lives is part of water. We are born, grow, mature, reproduce, die, and are repurposed, redistributed, and resurrected just like everything else in nature. Perhaps Thales was right! The universe is part of "everything," and "everything" in it is part of the universe. "Everything" is connected and interdependent to conserve equilibrium: unity, peace, and harmony—balance.

## MACROCOSMIC AND MICROCOSMIC PERSPECTIVES

Describing the world within the Ptolemaic macrocosmic system, Giordano Bruno wrote in 1591 of the infinity of worlds: "We are no more center than any other point in the universe." From this perspective, celestial bodies are governed by the gravitational force of nature along a two-dimensional equatorial axis. This is our outer world.

Within the inner world of the microcosmic paradigm it is not gravity, rather the other three forces of nature (electromagnetic, strong nuclear, and weak nuclear) that influence the behavior of subatomic particles. As a result, subatomic orbits are not constrained to a two-dimensional plane and are three-dimensional. Isidore of Seville wrote in *De Natura Rerum*: "The world is primarily the totality of everything, consisting of heaven and earth. . . . In the second mystical sense, however, it is appropriately identified as man."[1] It is from the microcosmic perspective that Leonardo da Vinci drew Vitruvian Man, with its geometry, measurements, and spiritual and alchemical symbolism.

> *Consider the example of a point within a circle. It's a very ancient symbol used by cultures across the globe. It's a simple symbol representing many things contingent upon its context. In science and alchemy a point within a circle is a symbol for gold and the Sun. Another way of looking at is astronomically, as the Sun within the solar system. It can also represent a child within its mother's womb, man within the universe, the soul within man, or wisdom found within the mountain of knowledge. A point within a circle is a symbol that embodies the concept of the microcosm within the macrocosm, something very small encapsulated in something much larger.*

### Paradox

What is a man who does not make the world better? Perhaps our greatest challenges are not macro- or microcosmic perceptions in our quest for truth. Perhaps our greatest challenge is one that Plotinus grappled with: resolving the paradox of the many and the one within the complex framework of monotheism, finding that harmonious place between our inner and outer worlds.

## LEAVES ON THE TREE

The universe is part of "everything," and "everything" in it is part of the universe. Duality. Duality in nature is necessary to achieve balance. Macrocosmic and microcosmic, large and small, "everything" in nature, "everything" in the universe, is connected and interdependent to conserve equilibrium: unity, peace, and harmony—balance. As such, it is addressed in the Bible.

"And out of the ground made the Lord God to grow every tree that is pleasant to the sight, and good for food; the tree of life also in the midst of the garden, and the tree of knowledge of good and evil" (Genesis 2:9).* This is an allusion from the first book of the Bible to universal duality on a macrocosmic scale. In the last book of the Bible, Revelation, we find an allusion to the microcosmic perspective with a reference to man and his place in the universe: "In the midst of the street of it, and on either side of the river, was there the tree of life, which bare twelve manner of fruits, and yielded her fruit every month; and the leaves of the tree were for the healing of the nations" (Revelation 22:3). Here too we are admonished in the closing of that final chapter: "And if any one takes away from the book of this prophesy, God will take away his share in the tree of life and in that holy city" (Revelation 22:19).

Curious, the tree of life. Referenced only in the first and last books of the Bible, it is the alpha and the omega. The tree of life alludes to the duality of both macrocosmic and microcosmic paradigms in conjunction with the tree of knowledge. The tree of life offers us life paths contingent upon our choices (a priori, a posteriori, a fortiori, ceteris paribus) from the tree of knowledge. As such, the tree of life and tree of knowledge represent destiny and fate.

Destiny and fate are often misconstrued and misunderstood terms. Democritus was of the opinion that every event in the universe was causally determined by preceding events while Xenophanes claimed that we have no way of knowing for certain that things are as we think they are. Destiny permits us to be involved with shaping our life path through our choice of decisions and actions. Fate, in contrast, is preordained, uncontrollable, and final without choice or involvement. Arguably, in a

---

*All biblical references are from the King James Version (KJV).

broad sense, destiny and fate are the same, as are the tree of life and the tree of knowledge. The difference between them is one of perception.

Edwin Hubbell Chapin captured the universality of nature beautifully when he wrote "The universe is a vast system of exchange. Every artery of it is in motion, throbbing with reciprocity, from the planet to the rotting leaf. The vapor climbs the sunbeam and comes back in blessings upon the exhausted herb. The exhalation of the plant is wafted to the ocean. And so goes on the beautiful commerce of nature. And all because of dissimilarity—because no one thing is sufficient in itself, but calls for the assistance of something else, and repays by a contribution in turn."[2]

### Autumn

Albert Schweitzer wrote: "At times our own light goes out and is rekindled by a spark from another person. Each of us has cause to think with deep gratitude of those who have lighted the flame within us."[3]

> It is the autumn of my life and I've experienced seasonal changes many times. My leaves too are turning color. Physically my hair is becoming gray, my skin is wrinkled, and I'm not as strong as I once was. I'm not able to do what I took for granted and did in my youth. Mentally I realize that my memory isn't as it once was either. Yet, in spite of the reality that I'm well on my way to that undiscovered country from whose bourn no traveler returns, I have endeavored, in spite of my foibles, to live a life worth living, to influence a positive outcome for mankind. My goal is to leave this world a better, more balanced place for those who follow.

In the movie *Kingdom of Heaven*, King Baldwin IV says to Bailian of Ibelin:

None of us know our end, really, or what hand will guide us there. A king may move a man, a father may claim a son, but that man can also move himself, and only then does that man truly begin his own game. Remember that howsoever you are played or by whom, your soul is in your keeping alone, even though those who presume to play you be kings or men of power. When you stand before God, you cannot say, "But I was told by others to do thus," or that virtue was not convenient at the time. This will not suffice.

The Hospitaller further admonishes Bailian that:

Holiness is in right action and courage on behalf of those who cannot defend themselves, and goodness. What God desires is in our minds and in our hearts, and what we decide to do every day, we will be good men—or not. Remember that.[4]

We seek truth. What is truth? "Truth is a battle of perceptions. People only see what they're prepared to confront. It's not what you look at that matters, but what you see. And when different perceptions battle against one another, the truth has a way of getting lost, and the monsters find a way of getting out."[5] Truth is as we perceive it within the construct and comfort of our reality.

As our lives culminate, what is important are the accumulated lessons we have learned and daily applying these lessons to grow in wisdom, strength, and beauty as human beings in the eyes of God and our fellow man. Ultimately, destiny and fate determine the extent to which we achieve peace, harmony, and unity of body, mind, and spirit—how we are repurposed, redistributed, resurrected.

Life: cherish it. But do not lament another's passing and release from terrestrial bonds when their corporeal time expires. Celebrate that they lived and that your lives touched. Remember, life is everlasting. They will be reborn in the spring and live again, as will you and I.

The Kingdom of Heaven is within us and all around us, not in mansions of wood and stone. Split a piece of wood and I am there. Lift a stone and there you will find me.[6] Gaze at the stars and you will see me. Bask in the sunlight and I illuminate you. Walk in the forest and I walk with you. Rest under a tree and I am you. May the God of peace and love delight to dwell with and bless you.

PART 2

BOOK

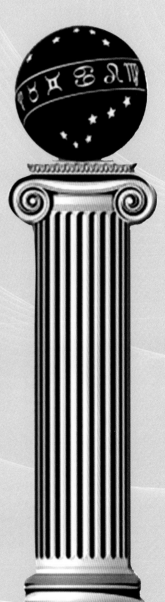

# 4

# THE PHILOSOPHERS' STONE

Richard P. Feynman (1918–1988) is quoted as saying: "Trying to understand the way nature works involves a most terrible test of human reasoning ability. It involves subtle trickery, beautiful tightropes of logic on which one has to walk in order not to make a mistake in predicting what will happen. The quantum mechanical and the relativity ideas are examples of this."[1] I'm confident this applies to the Philosophers' Stone as does his blackboard quote at the time of his death: "What I cannot create I do not understand."

Legends pertaining to the Philosophers' Stone are shrouded by the mists of time. Zosimos of Panopolis, also known as Zosimos the Alchemist, was an Egyptian alchemist and Gnostic mystic who wrote about it circa 300 CE. Other alchemists, such as Elias Ashmole, claim its history originates with Adam who obtained it from God. It is also alluded to in Psalm 118:22 of the Bible as the rejected cornerstone of King Solomon's Temple.

Zosimos described creation of the Philosophers' Stone as working with *prima materia,* or First Matter. The prima materia is the primitive formless base of all matter, sometimes referred to by alchemists as chaos. It is the material that fills the celestial world above the terrestrial sphere. Esoteric alchemists compare prima materia to the concept of anima mundi, the world soul, also known as the universal soul or breath of God. Anima mundi suggests that there is an intrinsic connection between all living things, as the soul is connected to the body. The process of working with prima materia is known as the Magnum Opus or Great Work. In the Hermetic tradition it describes spiritual transmutation as chemical color changes occurring in a laboratory. Ravens, phoenixes, peacocks, and swans are the birds symbolic of progression through the colors of black, red, and white aspects of the Stone.

The Philosophers' Stone is also referred to as the elixir of life. Symbolizing perfection and enlightenment, it is used for rejuvenation, to achieve immortality, and to turn base metals into gold. As such, the Philosophers' Stone is a symbolic alchemical marriage of our celestial mind to our terrestrial physical body bound by the energy of our spirit. This alchemical marriage requires change, transmutation, attained during a quest for perfection. Our quest is for unity, peace, and harmony of mind, body, and spirit so that in death our soul is resurrected to live eternally.

To comprehend the Stone, Masonry, the Bible, and life, we must have a strong foundation properly oriented in the seven arts and sciences, seven universal principles, Hermetics, and in the alchemical process. Acquisition of such knowledge removes the construct and constraints imposed by entrenched attitudes, beliefs, and values, opening our minds, changing us and our worldview. It's a process that opens our eyes and ears so that we may recognize truth in our hearts and have the experiential wisdom to be circumspect in its application. We must learn to look within ourselves. This is exemplified in the alchemical motto V.I.T.R.I.O.L.: *Visita Interiora Terrae Rectificando Invenies Occultum Lapidem* ("Visit the interior of the Earth; by rectification thou shalt find the hidden stone"). Another Latin motto used by alchemists when referring to the Philosophers' Stone was *mente videbar,* meaning "by the mind I shall be seen."

Ancient alchemists were crafty! According to the psychologist Carl Jung in *Psychology and Alchemy,* another of their mottos was *obscurum per obscuris,* "explain the obscure by the more obscure." Alchemists encrypt their quest for the Philosophers' Stone using metaphor and allegory. We find pursuit of the Stone described using a variety of cryptic illustrations and mathematics. Two examples are those of Sir George Ripley in what has come to be known as the Ripley Scroll and Count Michael Maier in *Atalanta Fugiens*. Ripley describes his quest for the Stone using symbolic illustrations. In contrast, Maier's approach uses sacred geometry. It is Maier's illustration that we will examine in more detail here.

Count Michael Maier (1568–1622) was a German physician, philosopher, epigrammatist, and amateur composer. He was well traveled in the influential court circles of Emperor Rudolf II (who invested him with the hereditary title of Imperial Count Palatinate) and King James VI and I. (Maier also composed the wedding song for the nuptials of James's daughter, Elizabeth Stuart, to Frederick V of the Palatinate described as the Rosicrucian alchemical wedding.) Maier is considered one of the great alchemists and Rosicrucians of his time. He had a strong influence on Sir Isaac Newton and is one of the only known alchemists to apply the canon to the musical arts. Among his alchemical writings are *Arcana arcanissima* (1614); *Atalanta Fugiens,* or *Atlanta Fleeing* (1617); *Themis Aurea: The Laws of the Fraternity of the Rosie Cross* (1618), which is dedicated to Elias Ashmole; *Tripus Aureus,* or *The Golden Tripod* (1618); *Septimana Philosophica,* or *The Philosophical Week* (1620).

In perhaps his best-known book, *Atalanta Fugiens,* Maier proposes alchemical solutions for creating the Philosophers' Stone using sacred geometry (fig. 4.1, p. 44). Accompanying emblem 21* is a metaphorical description of the creation of the Stone.

> Make of a man and woman a circle; then a quadrangle; out of this a triangle; make again a circle, and you will have the Stone of the Wise. Thus, is made the stone, which thou canst not discover, unless you, through diligence, learn to understand this geometrical teaching.[2]

---

*That Maier employed the number 21 for the emblem describing the creation of the Stone was not coincidence. The number 21 has significant numerological implications pertaining to the Stone.

*Figure 4.1. Emblem 21 from Atalanta Fugiens.*

Maier's description of the Stone is intriguing and often referenced. Unfortunately, it's deceptive, resulting in misinterpretation. It may not seem to make sense at first. It appears incongruent and unbalanced, but it isn't. Notice what he has sketched in the bottom left of the emblem: an encircled hexagram and a square adjacent to a T-square and compasses (in the form of a protractor).

Let's consider what Maier is conveying in terms of sacred geometry, numerology, alchemy, and Hermetics. First Maier says to "make of a man and woman a circle." What he wants us to do is to draw a circle containing a hexagram. When we use the compasses to draw a circle it creates a point in its center representing our soul within our spirit. The man and woman referenced are male and female triangles that comprise a hexagram. Drawn within the bounds of a circle the point within the circle is also centered within the hexagram. This point represents man's soul contained within his celestial mind that can change, encircled by his spirit, his character. Then Maier has us place a quadrangle around the circle, squaring it. The square symbolizes man's terrestrial body, his physicality. In this configuration the spirit unites and harmonizes the body and mind to form man's character. Maier further directs us to place the squared circle containing the hexagram within another encircled triangle. In so doing we create three golden triangles. The first golden triangle encloses the squared circle. The second golden triangle sits atop the squared circle. The third golden triangle occurs twice and is formed by the two 30°-60°-90° right triangles (two halves of a golden rectangle) situated on either side of the square. All these forms are contained within the outer circle of the symbol.

*Figure 4.2. Alchemical symbol of the Philosophers' Stone.*

The ideas of regeneration, rebirth, and immortality have been pursued by learned people of all ages. Cloaked in metaphor and allegory these ideas have been sought as the physical and spiritual metamorphosis of something omnipresent, omniscient, omnipotent, manifesting as the elusive Philosophers' Stone. From a Hermetic perspective it can be argued that finding the Philosophers' Stone represents attainment of the ALL, of achieving enlightenment. Reflecting upon the universal principle of the mental, the ALL is a universal living mind. A mind is made up of feminine negative energy blended with masculine positive energy grounded by tempered decision and action. Therefore, the ALL is *emotion, thought, and decision of the mind translated into energy as action by the body.* The ALL is both the individual (microcosmic) and collective (macrocosmic) mind and body.

Mathematically we can express Maier's alchemical symbol of the Philosophers' Stone with equations that are symbolically contained within its two circles, as follows:

Within the interior circle of the symbol we have a point centered in a hexagram composed of two triangles: $1 + (2 \times 3) = 1 + 6 = 7$.

The number 1 represents the monad, the soul, the universe, the ALL.

The number 3 is referred to as a triad and its geometric form is the triangle. It's considered an esoterically majestic number as it relates to equilibrium of body, mind, and spirit.

When we multiply the triad (triangle) by the dyad (2 or male and female) we obtain a hexagram representing 6.

The number 6 signifies union, harmony, and equilibrium.

And $1 + 6 = 7$.

The number 7 is considered a sacred and perfect number. It relates to time, excellence, wisdom, and a search for hidden truths. It represents spiritual maturity after a cycle of learning. Seven, formed by $1 + 6$, the monad and hexagram, suggests that the soul is found within a harmonious mind.

Contained within the outer circle we have a square and three different golden triangles: $4 + 3 + (0.5 \times 3) + (2 \times 0.5 \times 3 \div 2) = 10$. In simplified terms the equation is $4 + 3 + 3$, or $4 + 6 = 10$; geometrically a quadrangle (4 = the body) and a hexagram (6 = harmony) that add up to 10 (perfection). In other words, perfection is a harmonized body.

In numerology 10 is considered the perfect number as a 1 and a 0 together signifies the beginning and the end, alpha and omega.

If we look closely at the emblem we see that the triangle and square create an "A" encircled by an "O"; "AO" is alpha and omega. Together, these equations suggest that perfection of a harmonized body contains a harmonized mind and a soul bound by the circles of perfected spirit. The ALL is also represented by the number 13, a numerologically hidden number. In numerology 13 is reduced as $1 + 3 = 4$, ergo, the monad (1 = point/soul) plus the triad (3 = triangle/mind) equal the quadrilateral (4 = square/body).

In a geometric sense this is interpreted as an entity that is composed of a point, triangle, and a square. Again, man is composed of a mind and body containing his soul bound by his spirit.

In numerology 1 represents the male principle and raw energy. The number 3 represents the triad of the mind, the union of male and female creating a third entity. So $1 + 3$ are symbolized geometrically then as a point within an upward pointing male triangle.

An entity (1) plus a union of three entities (3) equates to 4 entities. The number 4 denotes a quadrilateral in geometry. In numerology it symbolizes stability. As such, the number 13 is a triangle in its essence, a quadrilateral in its quality. We find this represented in a square divided into four isosceles right triangles as in a pyramid viewed from above in the 47th problem of Euclid, and as a pyramid contained within a cube.

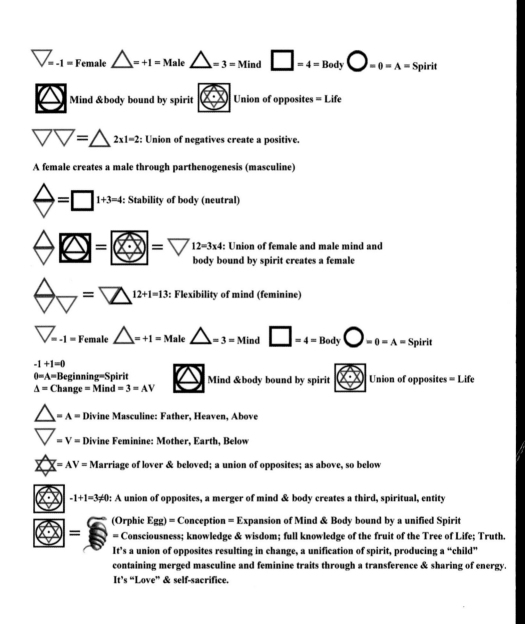

*Figure 4.3. Symbols broken apart and placed together.*

What Maier is suggesting in his emblem 21 is that by changing our thoughts and deeds as individuals (microcosm), humankind's collective soul, our character, is influenced and changed (macrocosm). Therefore, we are admonished to be circumspect in decision and deed as these define our character individually and collectively. When considered in this light, we find that Maier's emblem is geometrically balanced. It conforms with Hermetic principles and is alchemically sound in its geometrical and numerological translation. According to Maier the Philosophers' Stone therefore symbolizes enlightenment.

# 5
# AN OBLONG SQUARE

What do we know about the Philosophers' Stone? We know its name. The word *philosopher* comes from Greek and literally means "Philo's wisdom." So, we know it has something to do with wisdom. In general, a stone is defined as a hard substance formed of mineral matter that can be shaped for building or carving. Therefore, the name Philosophers' Stone could allude to shaping the wisdom of one's body and mind as addressed in Freemasonry. We know that working with the Stone involves the elements of fire, water, earth, air, and spirit in three stages alluded to in the colors of black, red, and white. We also know that the Stone involves geometric forms such as circles, lines, triangles, and squares. Our challenge is to figure out how to combine what we know to develop a functional model that we can see.

There is a Masonic reference to a geometric form known as an "oblong square." Some think it alludes to a rectangle, specifically a golden rectangle. But perhaps it's something else, something significant with broad implications. Perhaps an oblong square is a master key that unlocks the mystery of the universe. Perhaps an oblong square is the Philosophers' Stone!

When we consider the term *oblong,* an ovoid shape, a geometric form with rounded edges such as a racetrack, comes to mind. A square by its nature is formed by straight, not rounded, lines. Logically then an oblong square must be a square that has rounded corners. But how do we compose such a form?

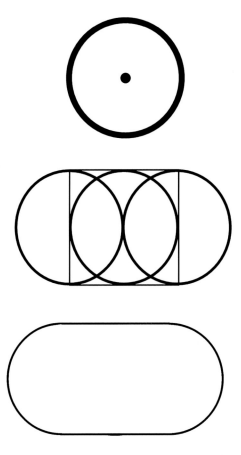

*Figure 5.1. Creation of an oblong square from three circles.*

In Masonry we are taught that "the form of a Lodge should always be an oblong square, in length, between the east and the west; in breadth, between the north and the south; in height, from earth to heaven; and in depth, from the surface to the center." The question remains: What is an oblong square? Whatever an oblong square may be, our Masonic description suggests that it's three-dimensional.

To create an oblong square, or the Stone, we begin with a point within a circle. We then square the circle and add circles on both sides. As a two-dimensional form an oblong square appears as a "racetrack."

Let's advance this idea of an oblong square through application. If we take our two-dimensional oblong square and make it three dimensional, what does it look like? Without removing the interior lines we have three spheres within a cube; a central sphere bounded by a cube conjoined by spheres right and left bisected by the cube. As a singular unit this configuration is akin to a capsule.

How is an oblong square applied to the Philosophers' Stone and Masonry? Let's look. Alchemists claim that the Stone is white and has dual aspects in accordance with Hermetic principles. The colors red and white differentiate these aspects. Red symbolizes the visible, physical, terrestrial, tangible nature of the Stone—our body, represented geometrically by a square. As such, the Red Stone is referred to as the "Lesser Work." The White Stone is referred to as the "Greater Work." White symbolizes the invisible mental, celestial, and higher intangible nature of the Stone—our mind, represented geometrically by a triangle. The triangles found within the Stone aren't discerned until we connect the points of contact between the circles divided into fourths and the square, at which time we find a hexagram (fig. 5.3, p. 54).

We find all geometric forms and working tools an architect can use to design anything are contained within its body. Notice in figure 5.4 (p. 54) that the lambskin or white leather apron, common gavel, and trowel are not among the tools included within an oblong square's design. This is because they are terrestrial *working* tools, not celestial *design* instruments used by the great architect of the universe.

Another important consideration represented by an oblong square is the presence of the three pillars (fig. 5.5 p. 55) and three degrees of Masonry. The three pillars also signify three ages* of man: childhood, adulthood, and old age, or life, death, and regeneration. They also allude to Hermetics, alchemy, and the Kabbalistic tree of life.

We also find an oblong square symbolizes the five orders of

---

*The ages of man can be either three, five, or seven, depending on context. The oblong square incorporates each of them.

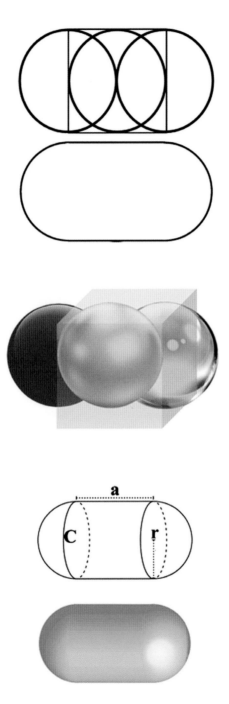

*Figure 5.2. A 2-D oblong square* (top);
*a 3-D oblong square* (center), *and a capsule* (bottom).

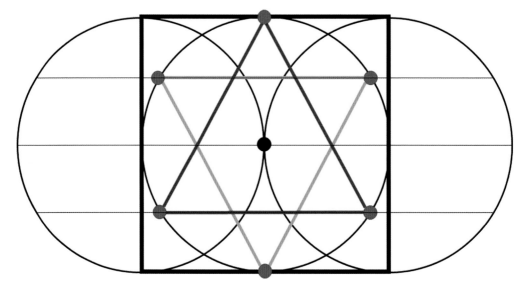

*Figure 5.3. An oblong square divided into fourths.*

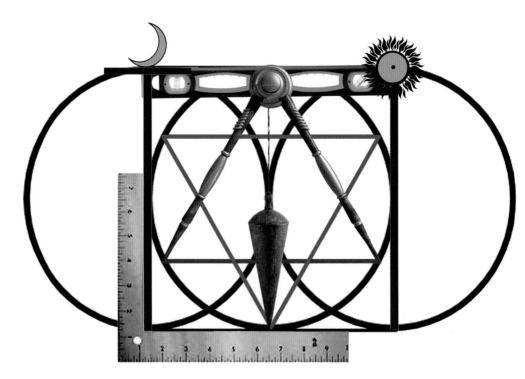

*Figure 5.4. Masonic working tools found within an oblong square.*

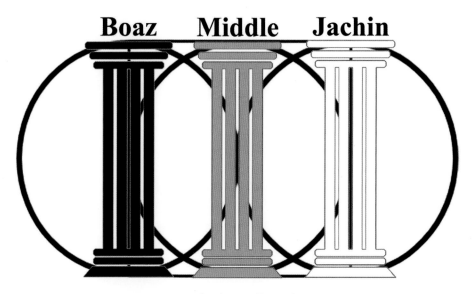

*Figure 5.5. The three pillars of Masonry.*

architecture, the five senses, the five ages of man, and the five points of fellowship (fig. 5.6, p. 56).

Further we find an oblong square correlates the seven liberal arts and sciences with progression of the seven ages of man (fig. 5.7, p. 56).

Let's consider how an oblong square pertains to the human being. The soul is an unseen point within the mind. The mind and body are bound together by the encircling life force of the spirit. The mind is composed of emotion and thought that create energy through decision, symbolized by the brain encapsulated within the cube of a physical body that expends energy as action in deeds. (See fig. 5.8, p. 57.)

Maier describes the Philosophers' Stone saying:

> For a Quadrangle of Four Elements are of all things first to be considered, from thence we come to the Hemisphere having two lines, a Right and a Curve, that is, to the White Luna; from thence to the Triangle which consists of Body, Soul and Spirit, or Sol, Luna and Mercury.[1]

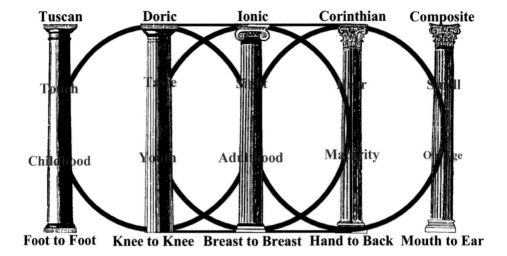

Tuscan    Doric    Ionic    Corinthian    Composite

Touch    Taste    Sight    Hear    Smell

Childhood    Youth    Adulthood    Maturity    Old Age

**Foot to Foot    Knee to Knee    Breast to Breast    Hand to Back    Mouth to Ear**

*Figure 5.6. The five pillars of Masonry.*

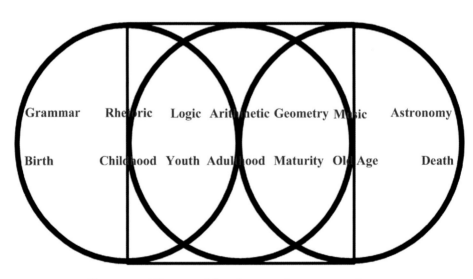

Grammar    Rhetoric    Logic    Arithmetic    Geometry    Music    Astronomy

Birth    Childhood    Youth    Adulthood    Maturity    Old Age    Death

*Figure 5.7. The seven liberal arts and seven ages of man.*

Is Maier describing an elusive oblong square? He references a quadrangle of the four elements, which would be a square. He then references a hemisphere having two lines connected to a white Luna, therefore a full moon or female circle. This would be a squared circle. The vertical lines of the square bisect the right and left adjoining male circles repre-

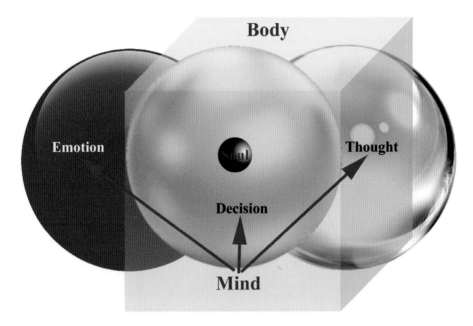

*Figure 5.8. Emotion, decision, and thought as mind, body, and soul.*

sented as the Sun and Mercury, creating hemispheres extending beyond the square. Within this circle is a triangle of body, soul, and spirit symbolic of the mind containing emotion, thought, and action.

Alchemically a circle symbolizes spiritual perfection, the unity and harmony of a perfected mind and body, our character. A point within a circle represents our soul protected by our character. An equilateral triangle denotes perfection of our mind, our thoughts, as celestial. A square signifies physical perfection, our body, as terrestrial. Considering this interpretation, Maier then is correct. The answer to the riddle of the Sphinx is not the deceptive *ages* of man, but man himself. Man is the Philosophers' Stone!

Man sitting in a meditative pose with arms outstretched, hands resting upon his knees, forms a celestial triangle. His physical body forms a quadrilateral terrestrial base. As Maier states, we are a triangle in our essence and a quadrangle in our quality. What this implies is that our essence is our mind within the quality of our body, that our spirit is defined by both mind and body as our character. An oblong square in its two-dimensional form refers to man's terrestrial perfection. If we extrapolate an oblong square as a three-dimensional form, man is encapsulated within a pyramid, within the center of three conjoined spheres, within a cube. As a three-dimensional form an oblong square refers to man's celestial perfection.

*Figure 5.9. Man as a pyramid within a cube.*

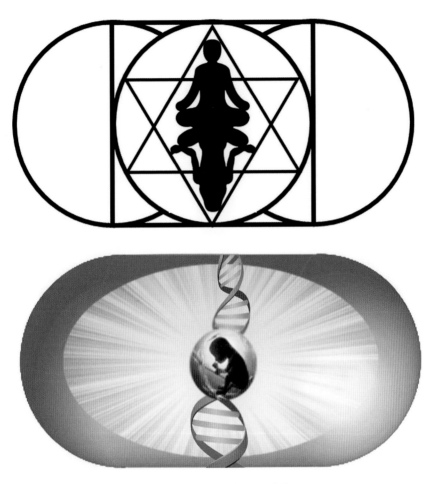

*Figure 5.10. Life: the union of masculine and feminine converts energy creating a divine spark within the oblong square of a capsule, a cosmic egg that manifests as a soul.*

However, to conform with Maier's suggested model, Hermetics, and alchemy, "man" refers to a hexagram where the female aspect of man is reflected in a union of opposites. Is this what Maier is suggesting? Could Maier's answer to the riddle of the sphinx and description of the Philosophers' Stone allude to the union of man and woman creating a divine spark, a cosmic egg, a conversion of energy, the manifestation of a soul—life?

## The Riddle of the Sphinx

Resurrection is a transcendence whereby we pass from our physical body and mind bound by our spirit to immortality as a soul. As such, knowledge and wisdom acquired through resurrection benefits—and is for—the living. Resurrection is often associated with and occurs during the spring equinox, a time of fertility, rites of passage, and esoteric initiation. As testament, the Great Sphinx in Egypt gazes eastward, directly into the spring equinox in front of the Great Pyramid.

In the Greek tragedy *Oedipus the King,* also known as *Oedipus Rex,* by Sophocles, Oedipus encounters a sphinx. The sphinx poses a riddle: "What creature has one voice and yet becomes four-footed and two-footed and three-footed?" If Oedipus answers the riddle correctly he may live and pass; if not, the sphinx will devour him. Oedipus answers: a man, because in the ages of man he crawls on all fours as a child, walks on two feet as an adult, and uses a cane in old age.

The foundation of the Egyptian pyramids is a square base, *four legs,* oriented to the four cardinal points representing the four elements. An upright triangle appears to have *two legs* supported by a *third leg* as its foundation as found in a pyramid. A pyramid is the physical union of a square and triangles as *one.* One voice, four-footed, two-footed, three-footed. It's a triangle in its essence, a quadrilateral in its quality. Could a pyramid also be an answer to the sphinx's riddle? Or, is the answer to the sphinx's riddle the "Philosophers' Stone"?

Referring again to the riddle of the sphinx in *Atalanta Fugiens* Maier describes the Philosophers' Stone, saying:

> What was answered by Oedipus is not known. But they who interpret concerning the Ages of Man are deceived. For a Quadrangle of Four Elements are of all things first to be considered, from thence we come to the Hemisphere having two lines, a Right and

a Curve, that is, to the White Luna; from thence to the Triangle which consists of Body, Soul and Spirit, or Sol, Luna and Mercury. Hence Rhasis in his Epistles, "'The Stone,' says he, 'is a Triangle in its essence, a Quadrangle in its quality.'"[2]

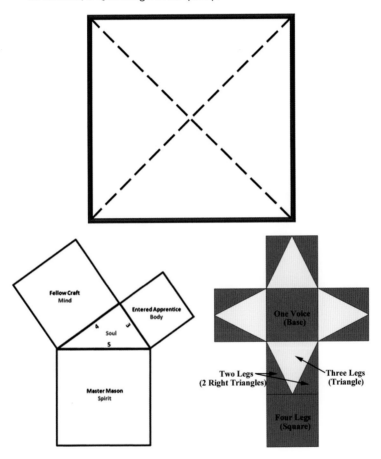

*Figure 5.11. A pyramid depicted as a triangle in its essence, a quadrilateral in its quality as an answer to the riddle of the sphinx. In a top-down view of a pyramid a square is divided into four triangles. As the 47th problem of Euclid, three squares form a 3-4-5 triangle. A three-dimensional pyramid within a cube unfolded as two-dimensional creates a Latin cross containing the solution: the base provides four legs; two halves of a golden triangle within a square above the base are two legs; and the supporting golden triangle within that square provides the third leg. Unified and containing the seen and unseen, a pyramid within a cube speaks with one voice.*

Is Maier suggesting that both a pyramid *and* the 47th problem of Euclid that the Great Pyramid embodies are the Philosophers' Stone? Or is Maier alluding to the elusive oblong square described as the form of a lodge in freemasonry? Is an oblong square the Philosophers' Stone? Consider a pyramid unfolded in its two-dimensional form as a Latin cross from the perspective of early man. With that in mind, another interpretation of Maier's description of the Stone and the riddle's solution could be that they represent the conjugal union of man and woman to produce a child, that we are the Philosophers' Stone. As such, could the answer simply be man versus the ages of man?

---

# 6
# ELEMENTS OF THE STONE

What Aristotle called *Matter,* Thomas Aquinas called *Prime Matter.* Matter that Aquinas saw and that was tangible he considered to be a result of a union between Prime Matter and Form that he called *Second Matter,* known in alchemy as the *Body of Matter,* or *salt.* Later, alchemists improved on Aquinas's idea and changed the reference of *Prime Matter* to *First Matter.* Thus, in alchemy, we have *First Matter, Second Matter,* and *Form* that equate to *mercury, salt,* and *sulfur* also known as the *spirit, body,* and *soul.*

Given two like objects of different color and weight, an alchemist will tell you that there is one similarity and one difference between them. The similarity is that they're both matter. The difference is that they are two *kinds* of matter. Other perceived differences, such as color, weight, density, etc. are *accidental qualities* that revolve around one essential nature. Aristotle concluded that matter and form were two principles concealed in matter. In simple terms, the form of matter is that which is tangible and can be seen. While matter has mass and weight, it has no form or accidental properties. And while it can't truly be seen, it has the appearance of a cloud, mist, or vapor. It is this cloud that's condensed into a universal chaotic water, the principle of all things.

Salt, sulfur, and mercury are symbolic allegorical terms, not the substances available for purchase at an apothecary or chemical supply firm.

Indeed, these substances are said to have a thousand names. Timothy Hogan in *Alchemical Keys to Masonic Ritual* says:

> We also learn from FC instruction and cornerstone ceremonies of the corn, wine, and oil, or traditional Masonic wages, which in traditional alchemical symbolism and texts were said to be associated with salt, mercury, and sulphur, respectively; (corn represented the body, or salt of the herb, wine carried the symbolic spirits, and the sulphur of an herb was its oil). These are sprinkled on a cornerstone just as the compiling of the three principles of salt, sulphur, and mercury into a stone was said to be the creation of the Philosophers' Stone of alchemy.[1]

Again, we find that salt, mercury, and sulfur symbolize not only the body, spirit, and soul, but also as corn, wine, and oil referred to in Masonry.

## WATER

In describing the process for creation of the Stone two components stand out: water and salt. Water is a molecule composed of one oxygen atom and two hydrogen atoms. An oxygen atom has eight electrons orbiting its nucleus: two electrons in the inner shell and six in an outer shell. Hydrogen has only one electron orbiting its nucleus. A water molecule is composed of three interlocking spheres as is an oblong square.

Water is the largest, most powerful, and sublime elemental force. Water covers approximately two-thirds of Earth's surface and makes up approximately two-thirds of an adult human body. Our bodies require water to function and survive. In the brain water is needed to manufacture hormones and neurotransmitters. Water allows our body's cells to grow and reproduce. It is used to deliver oxygen throughout the body, as well as for digestion, regulation of body temperature, flushing waste, lubrication, and shock absorption.

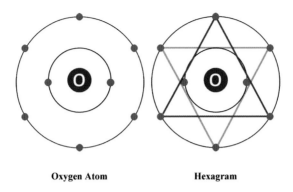

**Oxygen Atom**               **Hexagram**

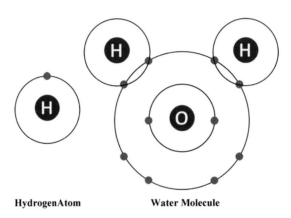

**HydrogenAtom**              **Water Molecule**

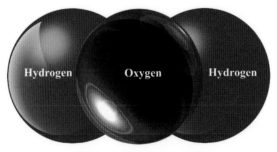

**3-D Water Molecule Lateral View**

*Figure 6.1. Components of a water molecule as well its
2-D and 3-D representations.*

Water is cyclical, existing in the three states of the alchemical recipe for the Philosophers' Stone: solid, liquid, and gas. Water rises into the air above the Earth as a gas and returns to Earth below as either a liquid or solid precipitant. As such it is found coming from the heavens above as rain and snow and emanating from the ground below as springs and streams. Water binds the terrestrial to the celestial. In the way it changes forms and cycles through the environment, it exemplifies AΩA. In the human body water is comparably consumed, circulated within, and expelled without.

Oceans are bodies of water that cover the Earth. The oceans are where life began on Earth. We gestate in and are born of a body of water. Water satisfies the Hermetic axiom: "As within, so without, as above, so below." Water has no beginning or end. Water is part of life, life is part of water. Water is life! As life, water symbolizes the universal principle of the ALL: "The ALL is part of everything, everything is part of the ALL."

Having three components and existing in three states, water is represented by a downward triangle. The energy required for water to exist in its three states is influenced by the element of fire. Fire is represented by an upward triangle formed by the triad of heat, fuel, and oxygen. Oxygen binds water and fire, as can be exemplified in a hexagram created by the electrons of water's atomic structure. It's interesting that hydrogen is extremely flammable, and oxygen is an accelerant, yet when combined they form a third entity that doesn't burn and can extinguish its individual components. Esoterically we could say that a water molecule is the monad plus the dyad that creates the triad. Thus we have a downward female triangle as water, interlaced with an upward male triangle as fire—a union of opposites.

Nicholas Flammel tells us what the Stone is in his *Alchemical Hieroglyphics* when he writes:

Our Stone hath semblably to a man, a Body, Soul, and Spirit.
I would only that thou note well, that as a man endued with a Body,

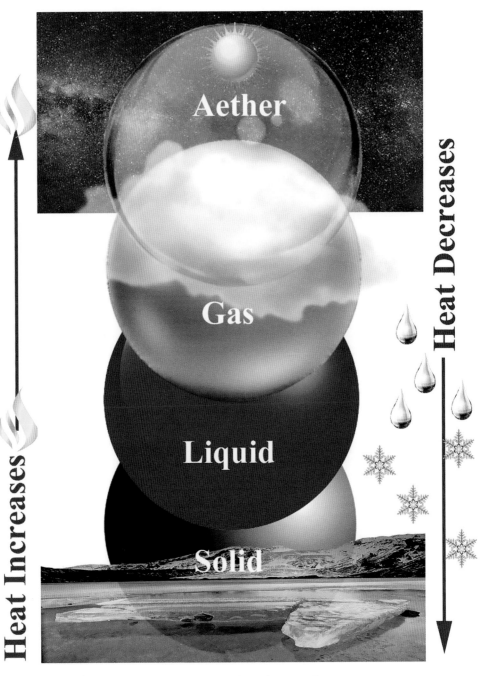

*Figure 6.2. The cycle and states of water.*

Soul, and Spirit, is notwithstanding but one; so likewise thou hast now but one only white confection, in the which nevertheless there are a Body, a Soul, and a Spirit, which are inseparably united.[2]

What Hermes, according to *Aureus: The Golden Tractate of Hermes Trismegistus,*[3] is telling us is that of the three, only the body is visible as the spirit and soul are invisible.

Understand ye then, O Sons of Wisdom, that the knowledge of the four elements of the ancient philosophers was not corporally or imprudently sought after, which are through patience to be discovered according to their causes and their occult operation. But, their operation is occult, since nothing is done except the matter be decompounded, and because it is not perfected unless the colors be thoroughly passed and accomplished. Know then, that the division that was made upon the water, by the ancient philosophers, separates it into four substances; one into two, and three into one; the third part of which is color, as it were—a coagulated moisture; but the second and third waters are the Weights of the Wise.

In the *Six Keys,* Eudoxus says:

There are three different substances, and three natural principles of bodies—Salt, Sulphur and Mercury—which are the spirit, the soul, and the body; and though they appear pure and perfectly united together, there still wants much of their being so; for when by distillation we draw the Water, which is the soul and the spirit, the Body remains in the bottom of the vessel.[4]

This too we find expanded on in a German alchemical poem, "Interpretation and Explanation of the Tabula Smaragdina Hermedis," published in *The Secret Symbols of the Rosicrucians:*

*. . . Sal, Sulphur, and Mercurium.*
*The Sal hath been one Corpus that*
    *Is the very last one in the Art.*
*The Sulphur henceforth is the soul*
    *Without which the body can do nothing.*
*Mercurius is the spirit of power,*
    *Holding together both body and soul,*
*Therefore it is called a medium*
    *Since whatever is made without it hath no stability.*
*For soul and body could not die*
    *Should spirit also be with them.*
*And soul and spirit could not be*
    *Unless they had a body to dwell in,*
*And no power had body or spirit*
    *If the soul did not accompany them.*
*This is the meaning of the Art:*
    *The body giveth form and constancy,*
*The soul doth dye and tinge it,*
    *The spirit maketh it fluid and penetrateth it.*
*And therefore the Art cannot be*
    *In one of these three things alone.*
*Nor can the greatest secret exist alone:*
    *It must have body, soul, and spirit.*[5]

Steve Richards in his book *Invisibility,* provides an excellent analogy:

Another way of looking at it is to consider the condensation of steam to form, first water, and then ice. . . . Water, steam, and ice represent what scientists call the three states of matter—liquid, gaseous, and solid—and what alchemists called three of the four elements.

Richards further quotes Albert Poisson who said:

In the alchemical theory, the four elements . . . are simply states of matter, simple modalities. Water is synonymous with the liquid state, Earth with the solid, Air with the gaseous, and Fire with a very subtle gaseous state, such as gas expanded by the action of heat. . . . Moreover, elements represent, by extension, physical qualities such as heat (Fire), dryness and solidity (Earth), moisture and fluidity (Water), cold and subtility (Air). Zosimus gave to these the name of Tetrasomy.[6]

With the above in mind we can create models of man as water and as an elemental form that includes the Red and White Stones: heart and mind.

## SALT

Salt, or salts, is frequently referred to in the Philosophers' Stone alchemical process. Salt is a compound created by combining sodium and chlorine to create sodium chloride. Sodium chloride dissolves in water and is what makes our oceans "salty." Salt is necessary for life and is found in the extracellular fluids of multicellular organisms. Since ancient times salt has been obtained through the evaporation of seawater to obtain sea salt or mining in quarries to obtain rough ashlars of rock salt. In ancient times salt was considered more valuable than gold, and alluded to as the white powder of gold.

Sodium and chlorine form ionic bonds. As a crystal these bonds create a two-atom-based cube three bonds in height, three bonds in length, and three bonds in depth—a perfect ashlar. In *Atalanta Fugiens,* Maier could be describing salt as the Philosophers' Stone when he quotes Rhasis:* "'The Stone,' says he, 'is a Triangle in its essence, a Quadrangle in its quality.'"[7]

---

*Rhasis or Rhazes (ca. 825–925). His given name was Abu Bekr Muhammed Ben Zakeriyah er-Rasi. Born near Teheran, he was a famous Arabian alchemist, physician, chemist, philosopher, musician, and poet.

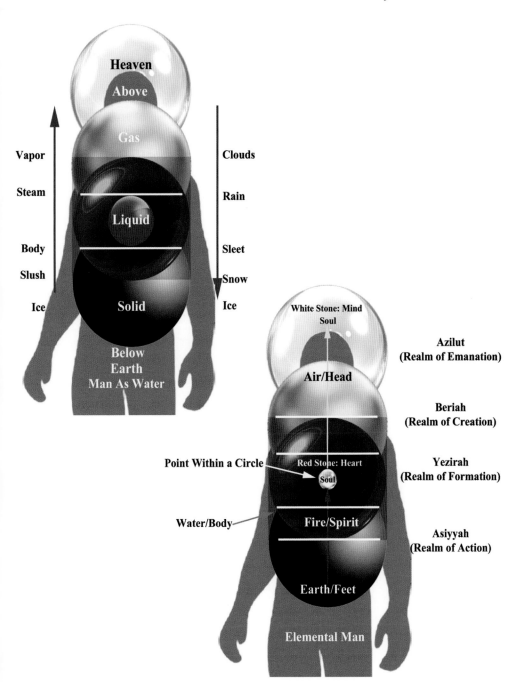

*Figure 6.3. Man as water and man as the elements,*
*which also align with the Kabbalistic realms.*

Indeed, a salt crystal is a triangle in its essence, and a quadrangle in its quality. When a salt crystal is combined with a water molecule it takes the form of an oblong square.

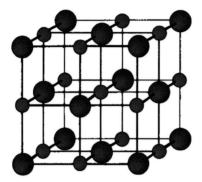

**Salt Crystal Atomic Structure: 3x3x3**

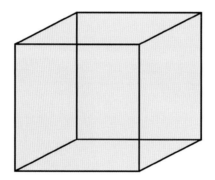

**Salt Crystal: Perfect Ashlar**

*Figure 6.4. Salt's crystal atomic structure forms a perfect cube.*

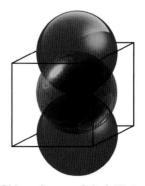

**Oblong Square: Salt & Water**

Salt dissolved in water isn't visible to the naked eye, yet it's hidden in plain sight. If water containing dissolved salt is distilled completely an experienced alchemist will find that a few small cubical grains of a white stone remain—perfect ashlars. An inexperienced person would not be able to see these stones if any water remained in the vessel during distillation. He would therefore unknowingly heave these stones over into the rubbish pile. Salt, like water, is necessary for life. It could be argued that salt is the Philosophers' Stone in a physical, terrestrial, sense; however, it lacks celestial connectivity.

A *hexamer* (six molecules) of water is the minimum volume required to dissolve one molecule of salt.[8] When dissolved, salt's molecular structure of sodium and chlorine separate to combine with water. In our body sodium regulates blood pressure by attracting and holding water in our blood. Muscles and nerves require sodium for the electrical currents they generate to properly function. The amount of salt in our body must be balanced. Too much or too little salt can cause health problems.[9]

One other fascinating aspect of a salt crystal as a cube: if a cube is unfolded as a two-dimensional form it creates a Latin cross, symbolizing life and regeneration.

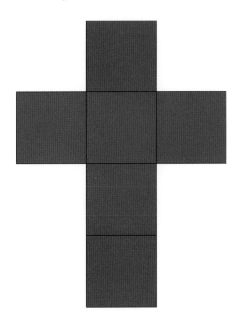

*Figure 6.5. Latin cross, formed by unfolding a cube.*

## CARBON

The combination of salt and water appear a likely candidate as the Philosophers' Stone, but there is another—carbon. A key component of life on Earth is carbon. The most important characteristics of carbon as a basis for the chemistry of life are that it has four valence electrons. Energy required to make or break a bond with these electrons is at an appropriate level for building molecules that are stable and reactive. Carbon atoms bond readily to other carbon atoms; this allows the building of long complex molecules. Complex carbon molecules also readily bond with other elements, especially oxygen and hydrogen. Again, we find reference to oxygen and hydrogen. For example, carbon dioxide is one carbon atom and two oxygen atoms.

In addition to its chemistry carbon's ability to conduct electricity varies with its hardness. In its soft base state of graphite, it's a black

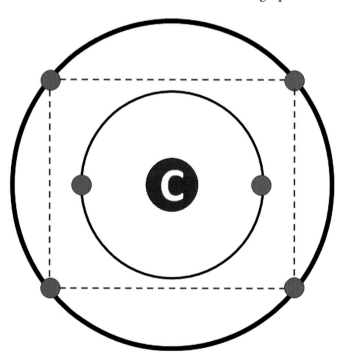

*Figure 6.6. Atomic structure of carbon depicting its four valence electrons forming a square.*

slab; this state is used in pencils to draw and write with, and it conducts electricity. In its hardest state as a diamond that is compressed by heat and pressure, carbon changes to a small white stone and is a very poor conductor of electricity. As such, alchemically carbon could be considered as a contender for the Stone since it begins as a soft black slab, changing color and hardness with pressure until it becomes a diamond.

Carbon's four valence electrons form a square, and its atomic number is six because it has a total of six electrons. So, while carbon has attributes of the Philosophers' Stone, it's not the Stone itself, nor does it singularly support an oblong square. However, carbon is part of the Stone. As with water and salt, carbon is necessary for life on Earth. Carbon appears to satisfy the alchemical process of the Stone. Geometrically and numerologically it also supports aspects of the Stone as it readily bonds with oxygen and hydrogen and forms a square. Carbon provides an explanation for having a fourth circle or sphere found in Kabbalistic, chakra, and Hermetic models. It also supports sacred geometry and numerology.

The Stone, therefore, is about life and is composed of life's three key ingredients: water, salt, and carbon. Again, without any one of these ingredients life on Earth as we know it would not exist. We can now create a visual model of the Stone that addresses the five elements and their interaction in an alchemical process that does indeed support Masonry's oblong square (fig. 6.7, p. 76).

Ancient Mesopotamians expressed the idea of the Philosophers' Stone representing water and salt, life and death, as an oblong square in reliefs. In the relief shown in figure 6.8 (p. 77), we see the oblong square in the center symbolizing the cycle of life as a fountain representing the universe.

In Egyptian legend an oblong square is also featured as the Philosophers' Stone. As one example, we find that the Egyptians used an oblong square to identify pharaohs as enlightened beings related to the gods by placing their name within a cartouche (fig. 6.9, p. 77).

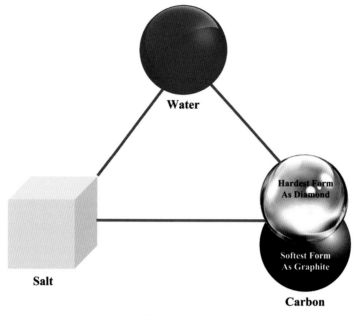

**Water**

**Hardest Form
As Diamond**

**Softest Form
As Graphite**

**Salt**

**Carbon**

**Chemistry**

**Soul:
Carbon as Diamond
or as Salt Crystal**

**Air:
Oxygen**

**Spirit:
Salt Dissolved
in Water**

**Fire:
Hydrogen**

**Earth:
Carbon as Graphite**

*Figure 6.7. A model of
the Philosophers' Stone.*

**Elemental Representation
as an Oblong Square**

*Figure 6.8. The original Assyrian alabaster relief wall panel dated
865–860 BCE is thought to represent King Ashurnasirpal II.
It was excavated from the Throne Room of the North West Palace,
Nimrud (Kalhu), in northern Iraq in 1846 and was acquired by the British
Museum in 1849. Photo by Osama Shukir Muhammed Amin FRCP (Glasg).*

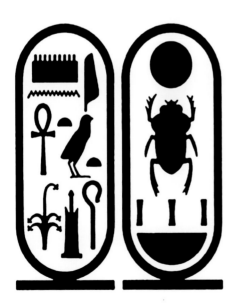

*Figure 6.9. Pharaoh's
names contained in oblong
square cartouches in Egypt.*

Cartouche

In the Hindu culture of India, we find an oblong square represented as a Shiva lingam stone. According to the *Linga Purana,* a lingam is a column or oval red and white stone that symbolizes the universe and the Hindu god Shiva. Shiva is said to be timeless, formless, pure consciousness, power, and the primal substance of all that exists.[10]

In medieval times an oblong square was used in floor plans for cathedrals such as the Cathedral of Notre Dame in Paris.

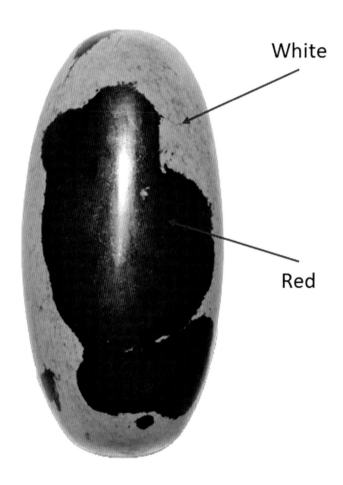

*Figure 6.10. Example of a Shiva lingam stone.*

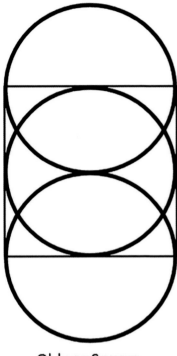

**Oblong Square**

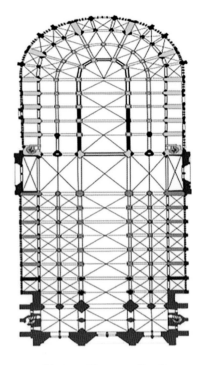

**Notre Dame, Paris**

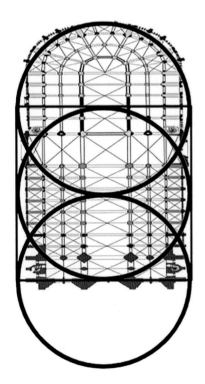

*Figure 6.11. Oblong square in the floor plan of Notre Dame Cathedral, Paris.*

# 7
# LIFE AND DEATH

## LIFE: THE RED STONE

Water, salt, and carbon are necessary for life. Without any of these three, life on Earth as we know it cannot exist. Together their molecular structures form an oblong square, a capsule. In nature an oblong square is found in the form of bacteria, eggs, and seeds. When an egg or seed is fertilized a divine spark occurs at conception manifesting a soul; this is when life forms. In this regard an oblong square, the Red Stone, satisfies physical principles of nature and Hermetics,[1] and the laws of thermodynamics.[2] When a seed or egg is fertilized, energy is converted and a soul is manifested in accordance with the first law of thermodynamics, the law of conservation of energy. The second law of

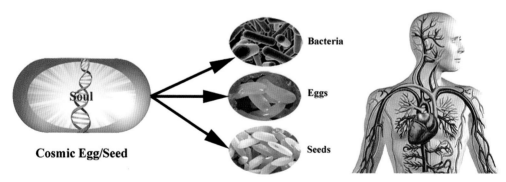

*Figure 7.1. Life as the Red Stone.*

thermodynamics, the law of entropy, says that energy disperses creating chaos. For chaos to perpetuate, order is required. Nature creates pockets of order through life. Life disperses energy; the more life, the better energy is dispersed. Life exists because of the law of entropy. Life as the Red Stone represents our heart and circulatory system, the first of our organs to develop.[3] Remember, we are first made a Mason in our heart.

Our heart is approximately 73 percent water, and our lungs are approximately 83 percent water.[4] Our blood, which is used to deliver oxygen throughout the body, also contains water. When we breathe we inhale oxygen and exhale carbon dioxide.

When we inhale, oxygen is taken into our lungs where it is absorbed into capillaries that combine to form the pulmonary artery leading to our heart. In our heart our oxygen-rich red blood is pumped in two beats from the left atrium to the left ventricle, exiting via the aorta to provide oxygen to our body by arteries that decrease in size to become capillaries. As our blood is depleted of oxygen and nutrients it absorbs carbon dioxide and becomes blue. These now oxygen-poor capillaries become veins that return to the heart via the vena cava where it enters the right atrium and is pumped through to the right ventricle and returned to the lungs in two beats. Our arteries and veins through which our blood flows form the Tree of Life (fig. 7.2, p. 82).

## DEATH: THE WHITE STONE

Our brain and central nervous system develop once our heart and circulatory system are established. A common expression that refers to the Philosophers' Stone is "heart and mind" or "heart and soul."

The White Stone, symbolized by the skull and spinal column, represents our brain and central nervous system, our mind. An oblong square encapsulates the celestial principles of mathematics, geometry, and vibration, and addresses the soul. In a physical sense an oblong square is emblematic of our skull (the white stone), brain (the three pillars), spinal column (the five pillars), and central nervous system (the Tree of Knowledge) (fig. 7.3, p. 84).

# Circulatory System

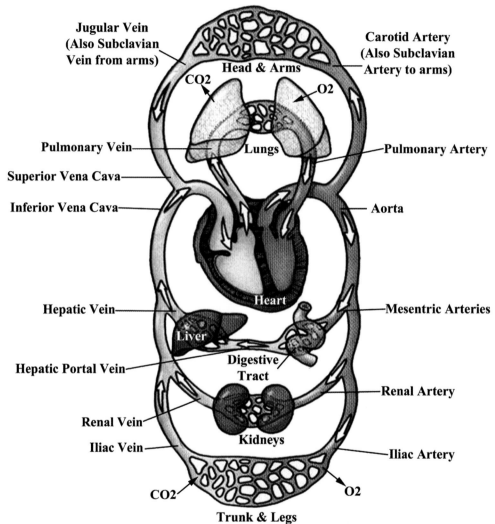

Jugular Vein
(Also Subclavian
Vein from arms)

Carotid Artery
(Also Subclavian
Artery to arms)

Head & Arms

CO2

O2

Pulmonary Vein

Lungs

Pulmonary Artery

Superior Vena Cava

Inferior Vena Cava

Aorta

Heart

Hepatic Vein

Mesentric Arteries

Liver

Hepatic Portal Vein

Digestive
Tract

Renal Artery

Renal Vein

Iliac Vein

Kidneys

Iliac Artery

CO2

O2

Trunk & Legs

*Figure 7.2. The heart as the Red
Stone* (top); *the circulatory system
as an oblong square and three
body systems within it* (next page).

# Circulatory System As an Oblong Square

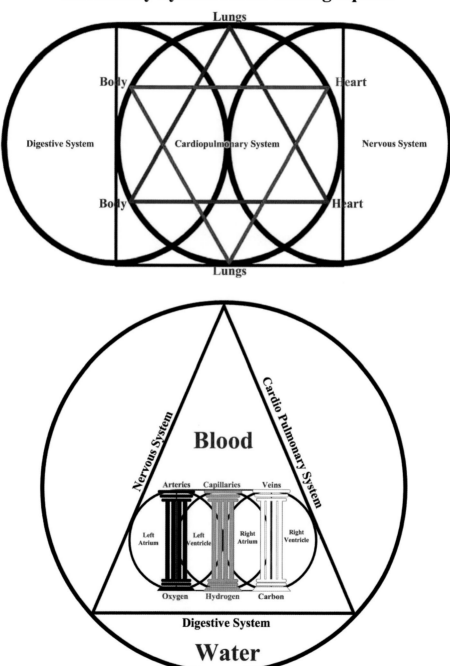

# The Skull
# (The White Stone)

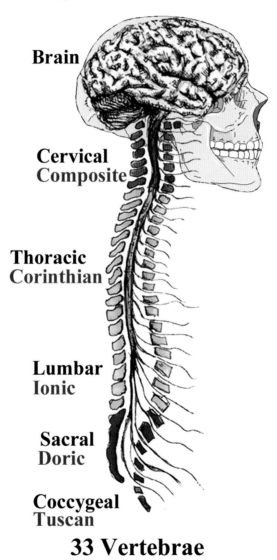

Brain

Cervical
Composite

Thoracic
Corinthian

Lumbar
Ionic

Sacral
Doric

Coccygeal
Tuscan

## 33 Vertebrae

*Figure 7.3. The White Stone as the brain and spinal column* (top)
*symbolized as Masonic pillars* (next page).

# Brain Structure (Lateral View)

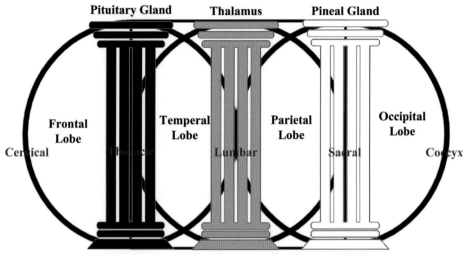

# Middle Chamber of the Brain

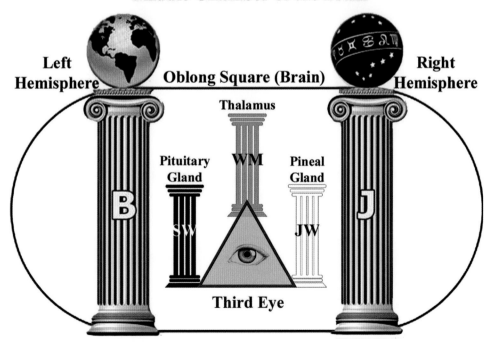

In Masonry, pillars and the oblong square are used to represent the brain and spinal column (figs. 7.5 and 7.6, p. 88). Further:

The pillars of Boaz and Jachin symbolize the left and right hemispheres of the brain.

The three pillars of Masonry represent the thalamus, pineal gland, and pituitary gland contained within the brain symbolized as an oblong square.

The five pillars of Masonry placed atop one another signify the spinal column.

In the context of the Fellow Craft degree the winding staircase refers to the spinal column, the porch is the brain stem, the middle chamber is the brain within the skull, and the sanctum sanctorum is the third eye comprising the thalamus, pineal gland, and pituitary gland.

When we overlay an oblong square and the Eye of Horus on our brain, correlations begin to appear in their relationships.

The Stone, via an oblong square and columns, is a path to resurrect and perpetuate our soul. This path, known as "the Way," is found in Masonry, the staff of Hermes, the chakra system, and the Kabbalah. The Way is found within us. The Way is a means of harmonizing our mind, body, spirit, and soul with the universe. Attainment of universal harmony, oneness, is referred to as enlightenment. An enlightened person is often said to have seen "the Light" or is depicted wearing a halo above their head representing light. In this regard the Stone is the celestial "elixir of life" that offers immortality.

Digressing for a moment we'll use some old, everyday expressions to explain the workings of the Stone. Are you familiar with the expressions "a fire in your belly" or "getting steamed up"? Generally, these expressions allude to an intense passion to actively *do something*. From an alchemical perspective we could say that we're applying the element of fire to our body, the element of earth, "warming our heart," so to speak. The effect stimulates us to action, and the element of water surrounding our heart

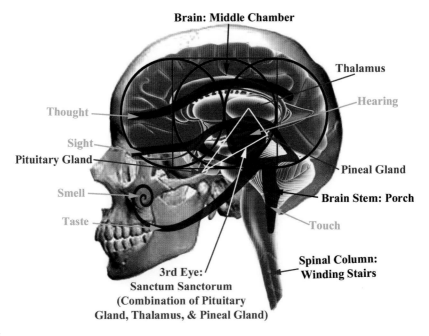

*Figure 7.4. Correlations between parts of the brain, aspects of the Fellow Craft degree in Masonry as parts of the brain, the Eye of Horus (overlaid in black), the five senses which correlate on the Eye of Horus diagram, and the oblong square (also in black).*

heats up until we become "steamed" or "boiling mad." This heated water, this *steam,* is *Second Matter* and "goes to our head," to the "nothingness, the space between our ears" where it coagulates as "brain fog" that "clouds our mind." This "fog," "cloud," "vapor," or "haze" is *First Matter.* It resides in our third eye roughly centered between the twin pillars, Boaz and Jachin, of the left and right hemispheres of our brain.

The union of opposites is a segue to metempsychosis as it relates to the union of the two hemispheres of the brain by the central nervous system, regulated by the pineal gland, pituitary gland, and the thalamus as an electrical system. It represents finding a passage between opposites and allegorically symbolizes finding the third eye between the two hemispheres of the brain. We can also see that it addresses the brain

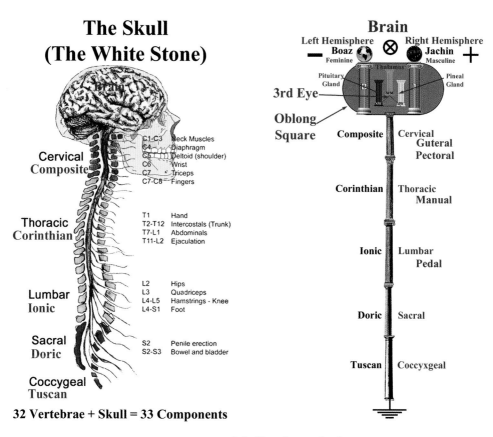

*Figure 7.5. Comparison of skull and spinal column anatomy
and the Masonic pillars.*

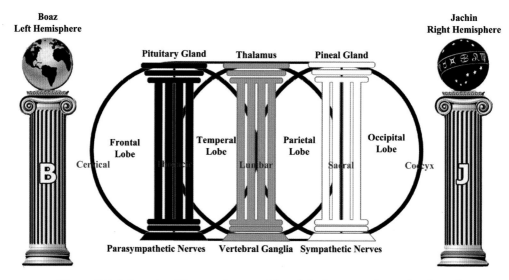

*Figure 7.6. Masonic pillars as the two sides of the brain with its glands and
lobes as well as the spinal column and central nervous system.*

## Correlation of a ship sailing between two pillars and pillars of the brain

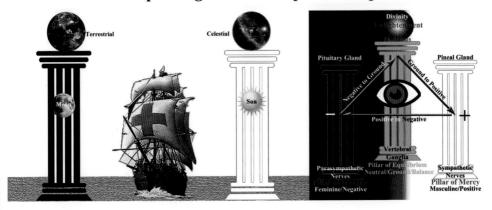

## Correlation of the Tree of Life and Chakras overlaid on a Caduceus

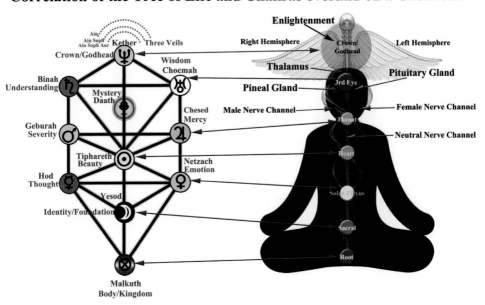

*Figure 7.7. The union of the two hemispheres of our brain and our central nervous system regulated by the pineal gland, pituitary gland, and the thalamus as an electrical system. A passage between opposites can be found that allegorically symbolizes finding the third eye between the two hemispheres of the brain. The lightning flash through the Tree of Life and as the chakras when overlaid on a caduceus also address the brain and central nervous system as being an electrical circuit.*

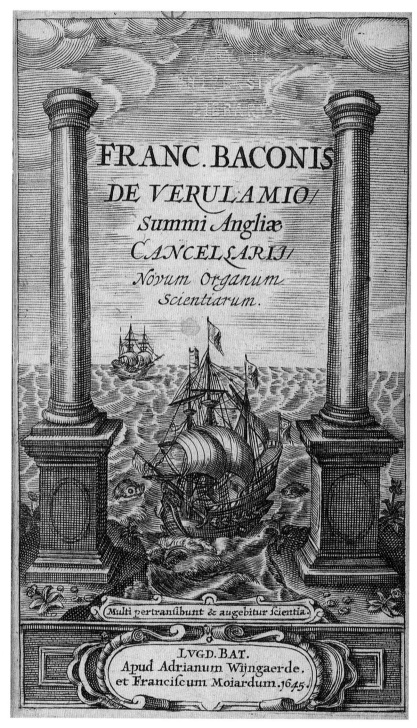

*Figure 7.8. Frontispiece from Bacon's Novum Organum Scientiarum, a book that presented an inductive method for scientific and philosophical inquiry.*

and central nervous system as an electrical circuit delineated as a lightning flash in the Tree of Life and as the chakras when overlaid on a caduceus (fig. 7.7, p. 89).

Related to finding a passage, the idea of a ship sailing between two pillars symbolizing a compromise between the polarity of hemispheres of the brain was introduced in Greek mythology's Jason and the Argonauts in their quest for the Golden Fleece as their ship sailed through the Symplegades or clashing rocks. Later the idea was incorporated by natural philosophers such as Sir Francis Bacon as a reference to the Philosophers' Stone.

As with the oblong square, the symbol of the Philosophers' Stone proffered by Maier shows the pillars of Masonry and our brain. Observing figure 7.9, note that there is a point centered within the

*Figure 7.9. Alchemical symbol of the Philosophers' Stone.*

interior squared circle and hexagram. It's located one-third the distance up from the bottom of the exterior circle. The center point of the outer circle is at the apex of the interior triangle where it touches the interior circle and the square. The center point of the triangle resting atop the square is one-third the distance up from the center point of the outer circle. These three points symbolize the pillars of Masonry and our brain. Symbolically the outer circle represents our brain. The large triangle is our third eye containing the thalamus (decision), pineal gland (thought), and pituitary gland (emotion). Notice too how the outer triangle laid over the square forms a square and compasses. The outer triangle also forms an "A," an alpha. When viewed in conjunction with the outer circle as an "O" we have alpha and omega, suggesting an end-to-end process.

# 8
# THE STAIRWAY TO HEAVEN

Now that we know what the Philosophers' Stone and oblong square are, the question is how do they precipitate change? How are they used to convert our mind and body from lead into gold? The answer is meditation.

Meditation is a vehicle for us to change. Meditation harmonizes our mind and body. Performance guidance for meditation is provided in the metaphors and allegories of Masonic lectures. Masonic lectures incorporate instruction for the application of Hermetic principles and concepts of sacred geometry. The Kabbalistic Tree of Life represented in the pillars of Masonry as an oblong square is symbolic of the brain and central nervous system performing as an electrical circuit[1] that correlates to the chakras as well as to the caduceus of Hermes (see fig. 8.1).

In Egypt Thoth was the god of grammar, rhetoric, logic, arithmetic, geometry, music, and astronomy—the seven liberal arts and sciences. He was a god of magic, medicine, and thought. Thoth was the scribe of the gods and their arbitrator in disputes. As such, he was the god of equilibrium. Thoth's Greek counterpart was Hermes. He was known for his speed and was the messenger of the gods. Hermes represents the speed of thought, and his caduceus, a staff with two snakes twining around it, represents the brain and central nervous system (fig. 8.1, p. 94).

The brain is the power source of electrical force, and nerves are pathways along which the electrical force flows within the body. Like

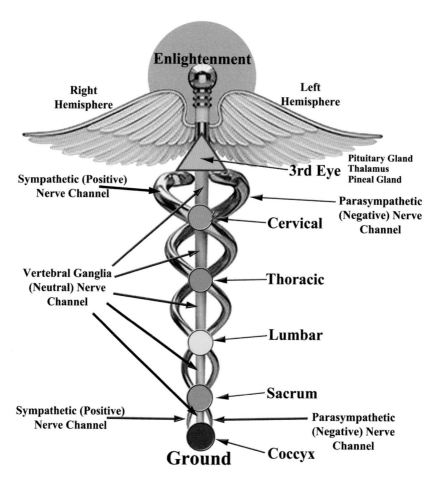

*Figure 8.1. Chakras superimposed on a caduceus,*
*representing the brain and central nervous system.*

an electronic motherboard, the brain regulates and coordinates all functions within the body. The brain's central processing unit (CPU) is made up of the pituitary gland, pineal gland, and thalamus, also known as the third eye or Three Pillars of Masonry.

The central nervous system (fig. 8.2) is the wiring harness that connects the brain to the body. It is made up of sympathetic nerves (positive, masculine, energy), parasympathetic nerves (negative, feminine, energy), and vertebral ganglia that provide a neutral return path

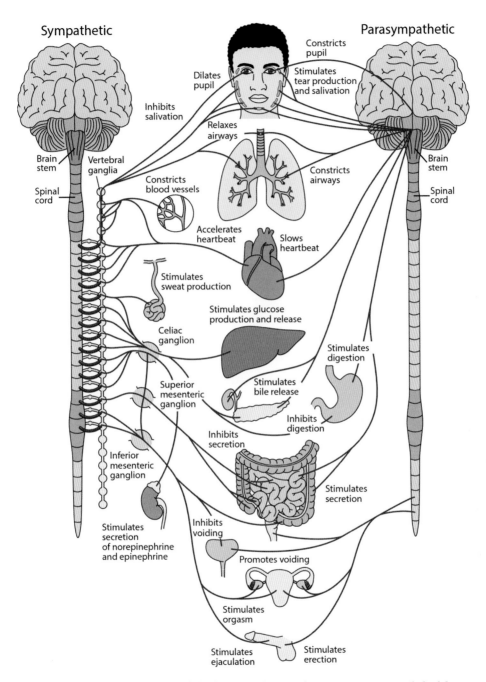

*Figure 8.2. Correlation of the brain and central nervous system with bodily functions. From the MSD Manual Professional Version Copyright © 2022 Merck & Co., Inc., Rahway, NJ, USA and its affiliates.*

to ground. Peripheral nerves from all parts of the body join the central nervous system along the spine where they are controlled and coordinated by the brain.

An electrical circuit processes and transmits information. A power source, our brain, provides electrons for the circuit. Because electrons have positive and negative charges, the movement of electrons within an electronic circuit creates energy.[2] Three principles of a charge created by electrons and their movement are voltage, current, and resistance.[3]

- Voltage: The difference in charge between two points.
- Current: The rate at which a charge is flowing.
- Resistance: A material's tendency to resist the flow of charge (current).

An electrical circuit is considered "closed" or "on" when its circuit is complete and uninterrupted. It is "open" or "off" if there is a break in the circuit. For a circuit to operate correctly it must be closed and the amount of voltage, current, and resistance balanced so that positive and negative electrons flow properly into a component (such as a lamp) in accordance with its tolerance and back out along a neutral route to ground. When a lamp is illuminated by an electrical circuit it emits photons that we perceive as visible light.

Electronic circuits use components such as inductors, capacitors, and resistors to tune and balance a circuit so that it functions efficiently at optimum vibration.[4]

- Inductor: A passive electronic component that provides equilibrium.
- Capacitor: An electronic component that stores energy.
- Resistor: An electronic component that regulates the flow of electrical current.

An inductor provides a capacitor with a constant charge, while the resistor reduces decay of the current flowing to the inductor. Together

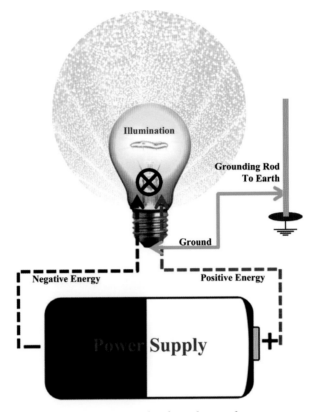

*Figure 8.3. Example of an electrical circuit.*

they create resonance, an electromagnetic frequency that vibrates. When such a circuit is tuned and balanced so that it functions at optimum vibration it becomes a simple harmonic oscillator[5] that generates electrical waveforms (fig. 8.4, p. 98).[6]

Our brain represented as an oblong square is comparable to the capsule-like shape of a servomechanism, which can be defined as a feedback-control system in which the mechanical position of an object is automatically maintained[7] using error-sensing feedback to correct the action of a mechanism. An example of a servomechanism is an automatic navigation system on a ship at sea. Servomechanisms usually include a built-in encoder to ensure the output is achieving the desired effect. A harmonic generator is a component of the encoder.

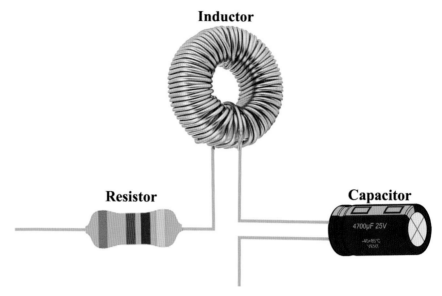

*Figure 8.4. Harmonic waveform generator circuit.*

Our brain functions as a servomechanism—like a thermostat that automatically regulates the temperature of your home. Our brain is our power source of electrical force, while our nerves act as the wires along which the electrical force flows within our body. As a harmonic generator, our brain's third eye—thalamus, pineal gland, and pituitary gland—regulates and coordinates all functions within the body (fig. 8.5). Our brain uses the feedback of these three to adjust the system, just like a servomechanism.

The thalamus[8] performs as an inductor controlling consciousness and sensory and motor signals and works to maintain equilibrium—or *decision*. The pineal gland[9] acts as a capacitor to store and modulate patterns and rhythms—or *thought*. The pituitary gland[10] functions as a resistor regulating the flow of physiological and psychological processes—or *emotion*.

As a triad, these components—the thalamus, pineal, and pituitary—form our "third eye." We attain enlightenment when our third eye is balanced and resonates as a harmonic waveform generator, which it does

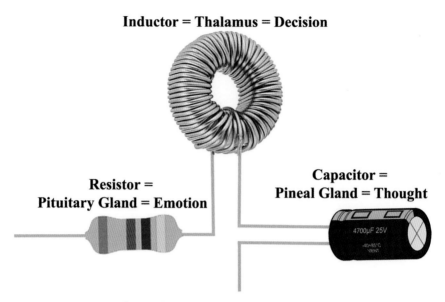

*Figure 8.5. Correlation between parts of a circuit and parts of the brain responsible for decision, thought, and emotion.*

at about 110 Hz. Opening and closing of our third eye is akin to opening or closing an electrical circuit (fig. 8.6, p. 100). It is simulated in the opening and closing of the Royal Arch degree by the words "we three do agree this royal arch to raise or close."

Our spine consists of thirty-three vertebrae divided into in five areas: cervical, thoracic, lumbar, sacral, and coccyx. If we include our skull, it makes thirty-three skeletal components. The spine corresponds to the Five Pillars of Masonry, the caduceus, and the chakra points and houses the central nervous system. Recall that the central nervous system is the wiring harness that connects the brain to the body. It is made up of sympathetic nerves that are positive energy, parasympathetic nerves that are negative energy, and vertebral ganglia that provide a neutral return path to ground. Peripheral nerves from all parts of the body join the central nervous system along the spine where they are controlled and coordinated by the brain. These positive and negative electrical forces crisscross through neutralizing ganglia of the spinal cord to various parts of

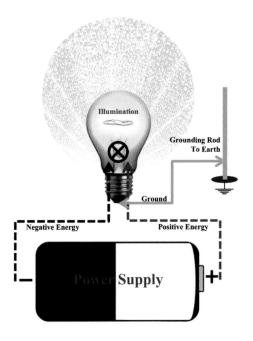

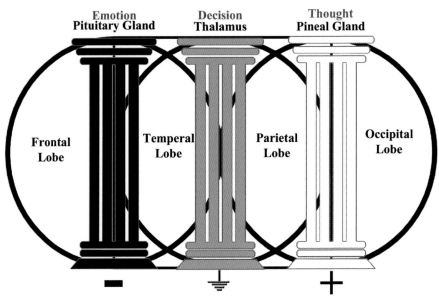

*Figure 8.6. An electrical circuit is formed when three parts of our brain—the thalamus (acting as inductor and responsible for decision), the pineal (acting as capacitor and responsible for thought) and our pituitary (acting as resistor and responsible for emotion)—form our third eye to close the system.*

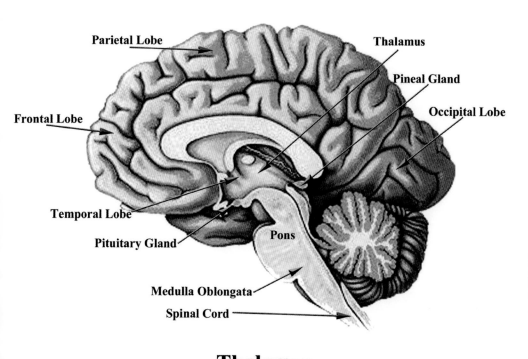

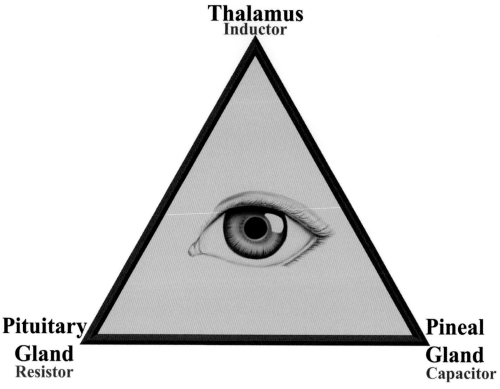

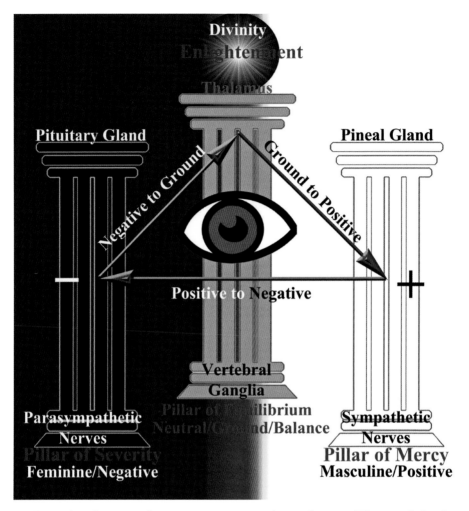

*Figure 8.7. Our central nervous system as an electrical circuit. The pineal gland provides a positive charge to the sympathetic nerves, and the pituitary gland provides a negative charge to the parasympathetic nerves. The completed circuit runs from the thalamus (ground) to the pineal gland (positive) to the pituitary gland (negative) and returns to the thalamus (ground) where it is discharged.*

the body. This is exemplified in the Kabbalistic lightning flash and the chakras, and is symbolized as a whole system by the caduceus. The completed circuit runs from the thalamus to the pineal gland to the pituitary gland and returns to the thalamus where it is discharged.

A vehicle for enlightenment is meditation. Knowing that our body is much like an electrical circuit, we now know that we must be grounded to benefit from meditation. We must be grounded so that we can properly conduct the electrical energy within our body. We must be grounded for our body's electrical system to work. To do this we must be sitting directly on the ground contacting our buttocks or sitting unshod in a chair with our feet on the ground. If we sit on a pillow or have something else between our buttocks and the ground it acts as an insulator and we're not grounded. If we sit in a chair wearing shoes it's the same thing, we're insulated and not grounded. If we're not grounded, our electrical system doesn't work properly, and meditation will be ineffective.

Nikola Tesla is quoted as saying: "If you wish to understand the Universe, think of energy, frequency, and vibration." Vibration is a universal principle. Vocalizing sacred words or sounds, that is, saying a mantra, is a crucial meditative vibratory ingredient. Vibration created by our vocalized mantra helps synchronize the rhythms of our body, mind, and the energy force of our spirit that binds them all together. A mantra is like a tuning fork: when tuned to the proper frequency our body, mind, and spirit vibrate harmoniously as one, much as a harmonic waveform generator does.

Meditation begins with relaxation and clearing the mind of all thought and emotion. The sound and vibration of our oscillating mantra emanate from our throat (guttural via the instructive tongue heard by the attentive ear), residing in the faithful breast (pectoral), traveling outward via the central nervous system to our hands (manual) and feet (pedal). It's the vocalization of the mantra, the sound and *vibration* of it, that harmonizes our mind and body. When our mind and body harmonize, our spirit harmonizes; we experience three-part harmony. Enlightenment occurs when we attain perfect pitch, experiencing four-part harmony of mind, body, and spirit synchronized with and resonating in our soul. When we meditate, we are tapping into a higher level of energy awareness, becoming one with the universe. Once we

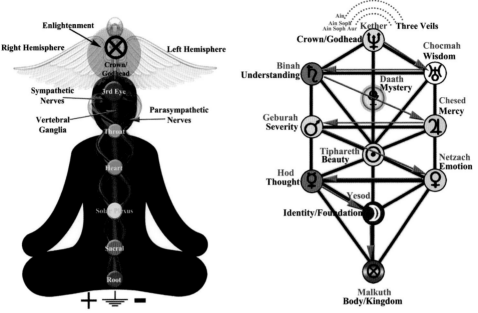

**Chakras & Caduceus**

**Tree of Life with Lightning Flash**

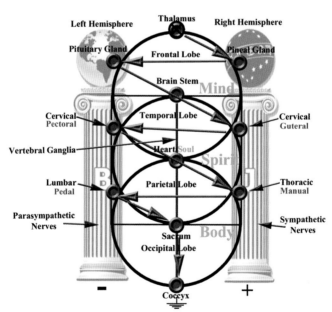

**Tree of Life as an Oblong Square
Representing the Brain & CNS**

*Figure 8.8. Correlation of the chakras and the caduceus with
two representations of the Kabbalistic Tree of Life.*

attain the perfect pitch of enlightenment we are not and cannot be as we once were. We are forever changed!

Many people wrongly assume that the brain's main purpose is in thinking and in storing information, but the brain does much more than that. Only 12.5 percent of our brain's energy is used for thought. In addition to encapsulating the 47th problem of Euclid and golden spiral, the Eye of Horus expresses how much energy our brain expends on our six senses. Interestingly, it expends the same amount of energy as described by its proportions.

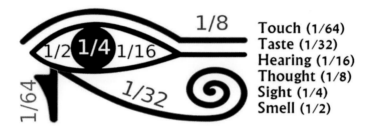

*Figure 8.9. The Eye of Horus expressing how much energy our brain expends on the senses.*

Together the thalamus, pineal gland, and pituitary gland within the brain are the source of electrical power and motherboard for the nervous system and bodily functions.

- The thalamus controls consciousness and sensory and motor signals—or decision-making.
- The pineal gland modulates patterns and rhythms—or thought.
- The pituitary gland regulates psychological and physiological processes—or emotion.

As a triad the thalamus (decision), pineal gland (thought), and pituitary gland (emotion) form the third eye (figs. 8.10 and 8.11, p. 106).

The brain and central nervous system are an electrical circuit. The thalamus acts as a neutral ground along with the vertebral ganglia, the

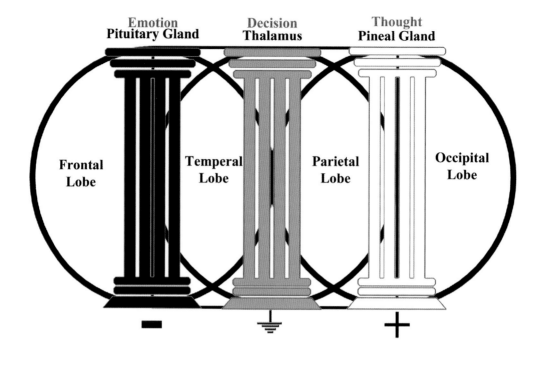

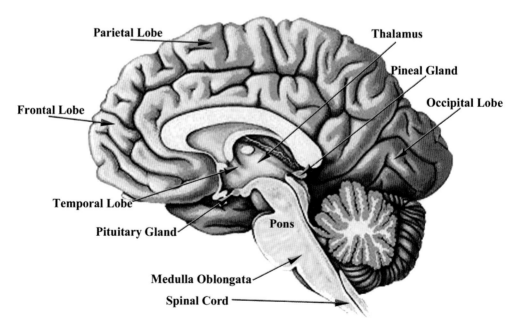

*Figure 8.10. The three pillars of Masonry as an oblong square and the brain.*

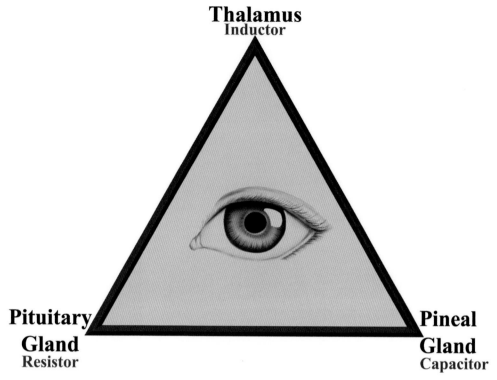

*Figure 8.11. The components of the brain that form the third eye,*
*which, when closed, completes an electrical circuit.*

pineal gland provides a positive charge to the sympathetic nerves, and
the pituitary gland provides a negative charge to the parasympathetic
nerves. The completed circuit runs from the thalamus (ground) to the
pineal gland (positive) to the pituitary gland (negative) and returns to
the thalamus (ground) where it is discharged (recall fig. 8.7, p. 102).

The chakras and caduceus can be taken to represent energy flow in
the body as an electrical circuit. The pineal gland (thought) provides a
positive charge to the sympathetic nerves from the brain down through
the five areas (five pillars) of the central nervous system within the
spine. The pituitary gland (emotion) provides a negative charge to parasympathetic nerves in the same way. These positive and negative charges
are neutralized and balanced by the thalamus (decision).

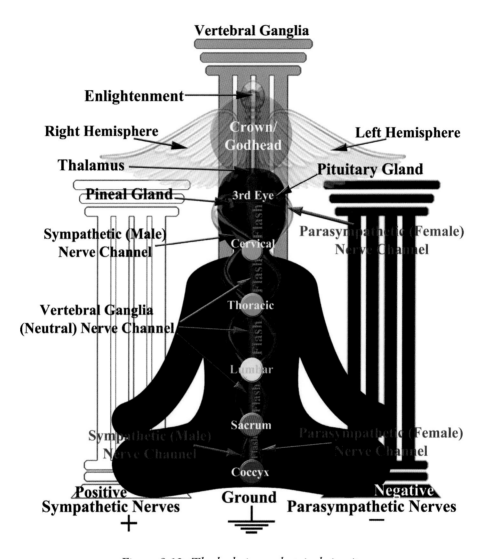

*Figure 8.12. The body is an electrical circuit,*
*as evidenced by the energy that flows through the chakras.*

As with the chakras and caduceus, the Kabbalistic Tree of Life can be seen to depict the three pillars of Masonry, which are themselves representative of the three pillars of the brain, sympathetic nerves, and parasympathetic nerves, as an electrical circuit. The charge, or flash, emanates from a point of equilibrium in the crown down to a positive

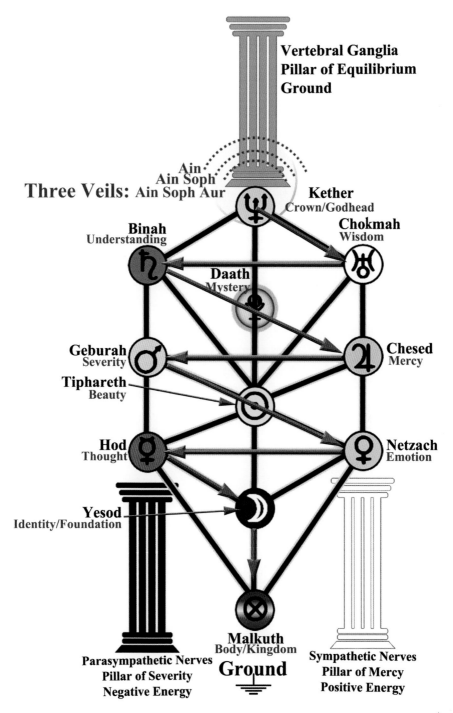

**Vertebral Ganglia**
**Pillar of Equilibrium**
**Ground**

**Three Veils:** Ain · Ain Soph · Ain Soph Aur

**Kether**
Crown/Godhead

**Binah**
Understanding

**Chokmah**
Wisdom

**Daath**
Mystery

**Geburah**
Severity

**Chesed**
Mercy

**Tiphareth**
Beauty

**Hod**
Thought

**Netzach**
Emotion

**Yesod**
Identity/Foundation

**Malkuth**
Body/Kingdom
**Ground**

**Parasympathetic Nerves**
**Pillar of Severity**
**Negative Energy**

**Sympathetic Nerves**
**Pillar of Mercy**
**Positive Energy**

*Fig 8.13. Lightning flash in the Kabbalistic Tree of Life.*

point in Chokmah, crosses over to a negative point in Binah, and down to intersect neutralizing Daath before returning to a positive point in Chesed as the charge crisscrosses the tree down to Malkuth and ground (fig. 8.13, p. 109).

For this flash to occur, body (Red Stone: three pillars of physical brain and nerves) and mind (White Stone: thalamus, pituitary, pineal) must be humming together in a closed circuit to reach spirit.

If we think about it, Maier's quoting of Rhasis refers to our body as the Philosophers' Stone when he says that the Stone "is a Triangle in its essence, a Quandrangle in its quality." The essence of our physical body, the Red Stone, is our cardiopulmonary, digestive, and nervous systems contained within the quality of our musculoskeletal frame. In addition, our heart is in the center of our torso, our faithful breast. It is the pump that provides for the flow of oxygen in our blood from our lungs and the exchange of carbon dioxide. As such, the Red Stone is concerned with the physical plane of existence represented by a square.

The essence of the White Stone, our mind, is the thalamus, pituitary gland, and pineal gland of the brain contained within our skull. Together the thalamus, pituitary gland, and pineal gland regulate and harmonize all bodily functions. Our brain, like our heart, has four chambers. Our mind, as the White Stone, has a higher function than that of our physical body. Whereas our body offers the stability of a quadrilateral, its functions center on itself as a physical microcosm. In contrast, our mind addresses that which is not physical and operates in the abstract spiritual plane of existence with a macrocosmic view. Our mind as the White Stone is flexible and subject to change, therefore it's represented as a triangle.

The Philosophers' Stone is about life, microcosmic and macrocosmic. Understanding the Philosophers' Stone is a mystery, a secret. Its secrets are hidden in its symbols, allegories, and metaphors. Of interest is that its geometric representation encapsulates the fabric of the universe, inclusive of a space-time continuum. It identifies a cosmic portal in accordance with the laws of physics, especially the laws of thermodynamics, that accommodates metempsychosis and regeneration of a soul. This portal allows energy movement without regard to the space-time dimension!

How do we enter and travel the portal? Meditation. Meditation is the portal to enlightenment. The vehicle that carries us through that portal is the vocalized internal and auditory vibration of a mantra that begins in our throat (guttural), is felt in our breast (pectoral), and radiates out through our arms to our hands (manual) resting upon our knees and then travels to our feet (pedal) and to the base of our spine that grounds us. Simultaneously we hear and feel the vibration in our head. An ancient mantra many are familiar with is "AUM," pronounced Om. AUM is found in the earliest Upanishads of ancient India and is associated with a mystical spiritual concept as a meditative tool. The three phonetic components of AUM (a + u + m) correspond to the three stages of cosmic creation, and when it is read or said it affirms the creative powers of the universe. AUM has been used by many cultures since the earliest times and can be found engraved in stone. Prior to the sixteenth century the letter *U* was not in written use. Consequently *U* was transcribed as a *V* in Latin and AUM was written as AVM instead of AUM. AVM is usually thought to refer to the Latin *Ave Virgo Maria* (hail to the Virgin Mary), used when performing the meditative practice in the Catholic Church of praying the rosary. So AVM is actually a reference to AUM and used as a mantra. It should also be noted that the secret word of a Master Mason also serves as a sacred mantra.

Meditation is the stairway to heaven, to resurrection and enlightenment. By perfecting our emotions, thoughts, and decisions we distill imperfections of mind, body, and spirit that encapsulate our soul, our character; this is symbolized as a grain of salt dissolved in water. We are altars of a sacred temple, a temple commanding reverence and respect, one meriting continual maintenance and improvement. Only with continual effort in pursuit of unity, peace, and harmony of mind, body, and spirit may we walk uprightly before God and our fellow humans. Only

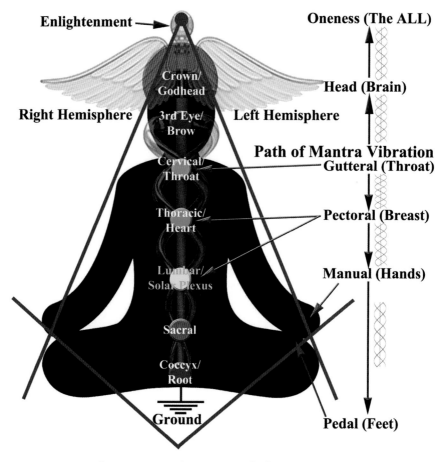

*Figure 8.14. Meditation using the secret word of a Master Mason as a mantra.*

with continual effort may we change our minds, deeds, and character. When we attain perfection we rise from the ashes of what we once were as a phoenix, the bird of Hermes, and become an enlightened ascending soul eternal in the heavens as the constellation Cygnus, as Apollo. We, each and every one of us, are a seed for change, an oblong square, a Philosophers' Stone—if we choose to be. This is what Masonry teaches us and gives us the tools to do, exemplified by the square and compasses.

# 9

# REGENERATION

In his book *A New Earth,* Eckhart Tolle writes: "The fires of suffering become the light of consciousness. . . . Suffering drives you deeper. . . . A lot of it is caused by the ego, although eventually, suffering destroys the ego—but not until you suffer consciously. . . . Suffering has a noble purpose: the evolution of consciousness and the burning up of the ego. . . . The truth is that you need to say yes to suffering before you can transcend it."[1] Suffering is therefore an element of metamorphosis and therefore metempsychosis. It's part of a slow, often painful, transition from one state of being or consciousness to another. We are born and must die if we are to be reborn as something different, conceivably better than we once were. Whether that death is physical, mental, emotional, or spiritual, death is a part of life and necessary for our rebirth. It's the law of entropy!

Before discussing resurrection or rebirth further, it's important that we understand how these words are defined. Resurrection is defined as "rising" again to life after being dead, the act of being resuscitated. Rebirth is defined as a revival, a second chance, or spiritual regeneration. It is a new or second birth that involves metempsychosis, meaning the passing of the soul at death into *another body,* whether human or animal. So, while resurrection and this narrower sense of rebirth may appear synonymous, their connotations are quite different. For example, when we say Jesus was resurrected after being crucified, what we're saying is that he was brought back to life from unconsciousness or apparent death, that he was resuscitated. When Jesus died, we also say that he was reborn, referring to his spiritual regeneration. What we ignore is the implication that at death his soul transferred to another body—possibly a human one, but it could be any animal, vegetable, or mineral. It's this transference of the soul—metempsychosis—that provides for life everlasting through reincarnation in accordance with Buddhist doctrine.

Reincarnation is an intriguing concept. There are several ways that it can be viewed. In one regard we could argue that when we are born, we are born in the image of our parents and our ancestors. At conception the energy of our parents' genetic makeup is converted through their DNA. We are a reproduction of our parents, created in their image, receiving half of our genetic makeup from our mother and half from our father. Our parents and ancestors, in theory, are *reborn* and will continue to live on through us and our descendants after they die. So long as we continue to propagate, our ancestors and parents will enjoy everlasting life.

Another way of considering reincarnation is using a clay vessel of water as an analogy. Let's say that you have a vessel of water. The vessel represents your body. The water represents your mind, your personality and life force, your spirit. What happens if you drop the vessel of water, and it breaks? What happens if the vessel has deteriorated with age and crumbles into pieces? The broken vessel at some point returns to the earth where it's repurposed. It might continue to deteriorate into soil, which later grows food for animals or plants or maybe becomes something altogether different. Ultimately it will become something other than what it once was. The vessel, our body, will not be in the same physical form we once recognized, but it will be repurposed and always continue to exist. This holds true for the water that was in the vessel too. The water doesn't cease to exist just because we drink it, or it spills out of a broken vessel. All water evaporates at some point, rises into the atmosphere, and returns to earth repurposed as something else.

It's a never-ending cycle! Water is our life force, our spirit. Remember, water *is* life!

Let's think about Egypt. The ancient Egyptians had a strong belief in the afterlife. They believed that your physical body (*akh*) contained your personality (*ba*) and your spiritual life force, your soul (*ka*). When you died, your ba and ka left your body and flew off. During the day your ba kept watch over and protected your family, and your ka went to the Land of Two Fields. So that your ba and ka could find their way home to your body, your tomb had to have your name engraved upon it in a cartouche. Otherwise, your ba and ka would be lost forever; you would disappear and cease to exist!

Picture a mummy in your mind. Does its sarcophagus/coffin have the appearance of a capsule, an egg, a seed? Yes, it does, representative of an oblong square. Now think about how a battery works. A battery uses a chemical reaction between alkaline and acidic sources to produce electricity. Our body does the same. During the mummification process organs are removed from the body. The body is then placed in natron (a very dry salt consisting of sodium bicarbonate and sodium chloride) and dehydrated. Natron is alkaline and removes all water and oxygen from the body, leaving carbon-based matter. The body is then wrapped in linen, anointed with oils that are acidic, and placed in a sarcophagus/coffin. The chemical reaction between alkaline and acidic chemicals produces hydrogen. Hydrogen has one electron and easily bonds with other elements. Its atomic number is 1. It's the most abundant element in the universe. In living matter it's found in conjunction with carbon and oxygen. Hydrogen is found in the oceans along with oxygen, sodium, and chlorine. So, we have the chemical composition of our oblong square as the Philosophers' Stone: hydrogen and oxygen bond to create water, sodium and chlorine bond to create salt, and carbon. Could hydrogen (H) contain the soul?

It is possible that the soul is encapsulated in a hydrogen molecule ($H_2$). Hydrogen is an energy carrier, not a source of energy, as it must be produced. This could occur at death if water electrolysis is employed, such as in mummification, which separates hydrogen from oxygen. It also explains the Egyptian concept of the soul as consisting of two parts, ka and ba.

Think of resurrection in electromechanical terms as being like the alternator in your car. When it's new it works great! Your battery stays charged. In time the alternator's brushes wear down until it no longer works, your battery doesn't retain a charge, and it dies. Your car is essentially dead until you repair or replace the alternator and recharge the battery, resurrecting it.

Life has environmental needs that must be met for it to sustain itself. Second, in accordance with laws of thermodynamics (conservation and entropy), energy cannot be created or destroyed, but it can be repurposed in order to expand.

Let's say we have a soul. In the physical world here on Earth a soul is conceived and contained within a physical mind and body bound by our spirit. If we consider a soul as a hydrogen discharge of positive and negative chemical forces, we become a battery discharging hydrogen in response to the cycles of nature. It oscillates as alternating current. Tesla was right! So was Einstein! But our linear concept of time, space, and dimension are relative only to man on Earth. They don't necessarily apply to "universal time" because they are man-made constructs applicable only to Earth's relationship with its sun. In that regard time is microcosmic and not applicable in a macrocosm of the universe.

When a union of opposites occurs, energy is transferred and merged in a spark of divine love, creating a pocket of order enabling chaos to expand in accordance with the laws of thermodynamics. A soul, a point within a circle, is formed, and life begins. We have an expansion of mind and body bound by spirit encapsulating a soul that grows as consciousness within the spirit of the universal womb. As the mind, body, and spirit age they deteriorate and ultimately collapse, resulting in death. The soul is released from its physical, mortal, bonds and returns to its primal state of divine love within the universal womb where it is reconstituted in a process of regeneration. This is the regenerative cycle of nature: life, death, rebirth. As an equation it's expressed as AΩA and symbolized as an ouroboros, representing Ophiuchus.

In contrast with rebirth, resurrection is for the living. It's a process of transformation, metamorphosis, that often includes pain and suffering caused by ego. Transcending our physical limitations through meditation we can experience the spirit of divine love, peace, and illumination. Meditation enables us to atone, destroy our ego, and bow our head to our feet in humility, allowing that energy to awaken the kundalini at the base of our spine and flow through the chakras as inner peace. It's a beginning without end, life everlasting, eternity that is a vehicle to achieve oneness with the universe. As such, much like the twin peaks of Mount Parnassus where we find the oracle at Delphi, the equation for resurrection is AA, signifying a beginning without end and life everlasting symbolized as a point within a circle denoting our soul and the navel of the world.

PART 3

CANDLE

# 10
# THE MAKING OF A SHAMAN

In part 1, "Bell," we answered the call and learned the historical back-story and foundation of the Philosophers' Stone. In part 2, "Book," we learned the operative mechanics, the concepts, and theory, of how the Stone works from a Hermetic perspective as imparted by a sixteenth-century alchemist. In part 3, "Candle," we will learn how to apply and use what we learned in the first two parts to achieve enlightenment. Our teacher is a contemporary Native American shaman. He will be our guide as we climb the mountain of knowledge, converting Hermetic and alchemical teachings into life lessons found within nature as we seek the flower of wisdom.

An adventure is sometimes far from the romantic notion of a good time. It can be a perilous predicament where one's life may well dangle in the balance. One wrong move or bad decision can end your life tragically and instantly. The only romantic aspect of a risky adventure is in its retrospective telling upon having survived it. The year 2004 was an important one for me. It was the year I was raised as a Master Mason, the year I converted from film to digital photography, and it was the year that I met Charles.

For as far back as I can remember I've always had an affinity for nature and exploration. During my youth I played in the woods, fields, and creeks like most boys at that time. We'd catch insects, spiders, frogs, snakes, and such. We observed and learned about plants. We experimented. We collected and crushed the translucent green stems and squeezed the juice out of a plant we called "juju weed." Actually, it was Jewelweed (*Impatiens capensis*). We'd rub the "juju" juice all over ourselves to ward of mosquitoes and poison ivy. It worked! Well, sort of. At least we believed it did.

I was also fascinated and inspired by one of our neighbors who was a birder. He erected mist nets in the woods and fields to catch, identify, and band birds. He described birds he caught in a logbook. On occasion he'd allow me to hold one of those delicate little birds. Holding a small bird in my cupped hands, feeling its frightened heart beating rapidly, I was impressed with just how fragile life really is. As the little bird squirmed and squeaked for release I was simultaneously amazed at its strength and determination to live and be free. Life—fragile yet vigorous—was a contradiction held in my small, cupped hands. Life was mysterious. It was beautiful!

In early spring of 2004 a neighboring town hosted a migratory bird festival. As I had become a birder myself, I was a member of a team tasked with finding good places to "bird" for the festival. One of the places we were invited to investigate was owned by a man named Charles. Charles owned about 100 acres of forested land on one of the higher ridges of a steep mountain. We found some uncommon birds, high elevation warblers, and secured his permission to bring birding groups there during the festival. Charles and I didn't exactly hit it off that day but found one another interesting. Since I lived at the base of the mountain I was more or less his neighbor, so he invited me to return the next day for a follow-up visit.

Charles was older than me, of medium height and build. He had piercing blue eyes—wolf eyes. There was something different about him, something about his mannerisms and the way he spoke. I would later learn that Charles was a Native American shaman.

When I met Charles alone for the first time I shared that I was recently raised as a Master Mason. His reply was along the lines of: "I know. My dad was a Mason. He wore a ring too. I am not. Masons are good people. You have much to learn." During that singular meeting and getting to know one another he said, "let's go for a walk." As we walked on the mountain he'd point out various plants and asked if I knew what they were. Many plants I knew, many plants I didn't know. He would then explain what the plants were used for and how to find them. As we walked and talked I photographed birds. At one point Charles asked to see an image of a bird that I'd just photographed. He didn't say anything. After walking a bit more he said: "You know, I don't much like cameras. I think maybe if you can capture the bird spirit, you know, maybe you can take a good photograph of just about anything."

Charles impressed upon me that as long as I was with him on the mountain that I was safe. He emphasized that the mountain was a very sacred place, that she had a strong spirit, and to respect her. He warned me that she would test me harshly if ever I were alone with her. For the next two and a half years I spent every opportunity I had walking the mountain with Charles. He taught me much about many things during that time through old stories. These were stories that were passed down to him from his ancestors and his teacher. He shared stories about trees, plants, and mushrooms; all of the animals great and small; water and clouds, wind and fire, the stars; creation, life, nature, and the universe—how it is all bound together as one.

In addition to his friendship, Charles planted seeds of knowledge. These seeds have taken years to sprout, grow, and bear fruit. They are still sprouting, growing, and bearing fruit. I'm still learning and growing. Early in our friendship Charles related a story about gardening and knowledge:

"I like to grow vegetables and herbs in my garden, you know. Some things I plant in springtime. Some things I plant in summer. Some things I plant in fall. The sun, the water, the earth, the seasons, they decide how long it takes a seed to grow, you know, to grow to make the fruit. Not all seeds I plant will grow. Even when everything is right they might not grow. If I plant them in the wrong season, the seeds, they won't come up. If the seeds, they do come up, the plants, maybe they don't grow right and maybe they die without making the fruit. Or maybe their fruit is bad, you know. Plants that are the same and planted at the same time, they don't grow and make their fruit together. Ideas are like seeds, you know. Some ideas, they come up, they grow, and they make their fruit of knowledge pretty quick. You know, kinda like a strawberry. Some ideas, they take many years to grow big and make their fruit of knowledge. You know, kinda like an oak tree. Sometimes ideas are planted at a bad time. Sometimes maybe they don't see the sun. Sometimes maybe they don't get the water. Or sometimes maybe they are planted in bad ground, you know. Maybe these ideas, they can die without making the fruit of knowledge. Maybe if these ideas, they make this fruit, this knowledge, maybe it is bad, you know. Maybe these bad ideas are sick with a poison and make other ideas sick. Some ideas, they never grow to make the knowledge even when everything is right for them. It happens like this sometimes. We must accept such things. This I cannot explain."

If you are reading this book, it is because it has come to you. Many ideas contained here you may know, many ideas you may not know. What you learn from it and what you do with the knowledge is up to you. The purpose here is to cause you to question, to think for yourself, to flex your paradigms and travel beyond your comfort zone—to encourage you to grow and advance. But to grow and advance requires death before rebirth. We must create order out of chaos; it is the law of entropy.

You are about to embark on an adventure, to become engaged in a quest for knowledge that you may know little or nothing about. Our quest is a journey, not a destination. It is a long, lonely, narrow path we tread, a path illuminated by little more than our hope. Often, we are beset by ruffians; incidents will occur. Remember in whom you place your trust!

Before you begin, turn your gaze inward. Ask yourself: *What is it I seek? Why do I seek it? How will I recognize it? Where might I find it? What will I do with it?* Visualize your answer; picture it in your mind!

There is a flower growing high up on a mountain. This mountain is steep, and it is dangerous. This mountain is sacred. She is old and has a strong spirit. She will test you harshly. You must show her respect. You must show her that you are brave and strong of spirit. If you are strong of spirit and respect her, she may share her secrets. Many have gone to this mountain; few survive her. Fewer still return to sing their tales of exploration and adventure. If you are duly and truly prepared in your heart, then go. Go to this mountain. Seek this flower.

## THE LITTLE SNAKE

In one of the most poignant lessons Charles imparted he used a little snake. It's a cherished memory. I can almost hear his voice as if it just happened.

During one of our walks in the forest on the mountain Charles stopped and pointed at a rock with his stick.

"There's a snake who lives under that rock. Lift up the rock and see if he's at home, I would like to talk with him."

Here we are in a dense forest, no path, on a rugged mountain with lots of rocks, and he's telling me there's a snake under a rock that he wants to talk to? Yeah, right! But I did as he asked and lifted the rock. To my amazement there was a small snake under it. Charles bent down and picked up the snake, which wrapped around his forearm. He said something to it that I didn't understand. He then thrusts the snake out toward me and asks if it's a boy or a girl. I couldn't tell one way or the other. The snake's forked tongue flicked in and out, and Charles says:

"Look at that, he has two tongues. I think this is why snakes are often confused, you know. They don't know if they are boys or girls, and they have two tongues. They don't know the difference between truth and a lie. They don't know right from wrong, you know. The snake he is nice to me right now, but maybe he will become angry and bite me. We don't trust the snake because he is often confused like this, you know. But the snake, he is important even if he is confused and has a bad temper, you know. The snake, he likes to wrap around things. He likes to hide behind things and hide under things. He will trick you if you let him. That is his nature, you know. But the snake, he is wise. He can show you which path to take if he thinks you're not looking. I am glad the snake, he was home today. I needed to speak with him."

With that Charles spoke to the snake again before releasing it. We ignored the snake, catching a glimpse of it slithering off. We continued our walk in the direction it had gone.

In the evening after our walk on the mountain when we encountered the little snake, Charles and I sat by a small fire in front of his lodge. It was a warm, beautiful night in early fall. The sky was clear with many stars. The flames flickered, crackled, and popped sending up sparks that kettled in the rising smoke. In the darkness, his face illuminated by the orange glow of firelight, Charles related the story of the giant lizard. In a hushed voice he began:

"A white-haired man, he took a group of young boys deep into the forest of a high mountain, you know. He took them to this place, you know, to collect plants. They traveled deep into the forest. It was a place that the boys, they didn't know. High up on the mountain it was. When the white-haired man, he and the young boys, they made their camp, he sent two boys to collect wood for the fire. He warned these two boys to be careful. He warned them to pay attention because they were in a dangerous place. There were many dangerous things deep in the forest high on that mountain, you know. He warned these two boys to be careful. These boys, they were young and did not listen very well to the white-haired man. These boys, they are in the forest getting wood for the fire when one of them sees a tree with a large hole in its trunk. He says to the other boy 'I wonder what is in that hole in that tree?' The other boy, he becomes afraid. He becomes afraid and remembers what the white-haired man warned them. He becomes afraid, you know, and he tells the first boy not to go to that tree with the hole in it. But the first boy, he doesn't listen. The first boy, he doesn't listen. He goes to the tree with the hole and knocks on it. A giant lizard comes out of the hole. A giant lizard, he comes out of the hole and grabs the boy! The giant lizard, he takes the boy into the tree. When the lizard, he takes the first boy into the tree the other boy ran as fast as he could back to camp. The other boy, he was very scared. He was very scared, and he told the white-haired man what happened. The white-haired man, he was angry that the boys didn't listen to him. He was angry because he knew the giant lizard would come for them. The white-haired man, he and the boys built a mound on the side of the fire where the lizard would come. They built a mound near their fire for protection from the lizard, you know. The white-haired man, he made a formula and put it on the mound. He put it on the mound for the lizard. The lizard, he came for them that night. It was a giant lizard! This giant lizard, he was going to eat them! But when the giant lizard got to the mound he tasted the formula with his tongue. He tasted the formula with his tongue and he left. For three nights the lizard, he came. Each night when his tongue tasted the formula, the lizard, he would leave. On the third night when the lizard tasted the formula he died. He died right there, you know, on the mound near the fire after tasting the formula. The white-haired man, he and the young boys cut off the lizard's head. They cut off the lizard's head and put it on a long pole. They took this pole with the lizard's head back to their village. Outside the village the white-haired man, he placed this lizard's head on the tops of different trees to see what it would do. Each different tree died when the lizard's head was placed on it. Each different tree died because the lizard's blood, it was poison. Each different tree, they died from the lizard's blood except for the cedar tree. The cedar tree, it drank the lizard's blood, and it didn't die. This is why the inside of a cedar tree is red. The inside of a cedar tree is red because of the lizard's blood. This is why the cedar tree is important. The cedar tree, she is a sacred medicine tree, you know."

Charles spat in the fire and began to talk of other things.

## IN THE BEGINNING

The first Friday of July in 2004 Charles informed me that we were going camping high up on the mountain. By late afternoon we had hiked several miles over steep rocky terrain to a knob on top of the mountain. Surrounded by still-blooming red rhododendron, we made camp. Our first order of business was establishing a circle of stones with a fire pit in its center—a point within a protective circle. After removing small rocks and sweeping the circle clean with cedar branches, Charles, now with red stripes painted on his cheeks, used a smoking sage smudge to purify our camp area. Using cedar twigs and branches we started a fire in the pit. At dusk we made the fire bigger. As branches crackled to life the large orange disk of a full moon rose in the east as the red sun faded to the west. Stars began to appear as swirling sparks flew up to meet them. Sitting cross-legged together by the flickering orange-yellow flames Charles began sharing a story.

"Tsoyaha are my people. We're children of the sun, you know. We came here from across the great water," he gestured toward the east, "where the morning sun rises. This was a long time ago. When we came here there were no people. There was only the Tsoyaha."

Pointing at the stars he went on, "Before we came on the great water we came to visit this world from up there. The animals and the plants, they came to visit too. Some of us we didn't stay. Some of us, we went home. On this day when the sun stays long in the sky we are close to them. Maybe they will visit again, I don't know. Some of us, we stayed here in this world. Some, they went to the lower world down there," nodding his head toward the darkness below our camp. "We had a good relationship with the plants and the animals. We helped each other. It was good, you know."

"Before this world there was only water. There was only water and darkness and wind, you know. The wind, it became tired and had no place to rest. The wind, it wanted a place to sit and rest. 'Who will make a place for me to rest?' said the wind. The crawfish, he heard the wind crying and said, 'I will make you land. I will make you land so you can rest.' The crawfish, he swam to the bottom of the great water. With his tail the crawfish, he begins to scoop the mud and make a pile. The animals at the bottom of the great water weren't happy about this, you know. The animals at the bottom of the great water, they wanted to catch the crawfish. But the crawfish, he made a cloud from the mud so they couldn't see him. The crawfish, he continues to scoop the mud until the mud it comes out of the water. The crawfish, he made the land for the wind to rest.

"The wind, it said the land was too soft. The land was too soft, and she couldn't sit and rest. 'Who will dry the land so I can rest?' The wind said. The little birds, they came, but they were too small, you know. They couldn't dry the land. Hawk, he came and tried to dry the land. Hawk, he couldn't dry the land. Turkey Buzzard, he came. Turkey Buzzard, he was bigger than Hawk. With his great wings Turkey Buzzard, he made the land dry. Where Turkey Buzzard flapped his wings he made mountains and valleys. The wind, it sat and rested.

"The wind, it sat and rested on the dry land. Then the wind, it said, 'It's dark. Who will make the light?' A little star said she would make the light," Charles pointed at Venus setting in the west. "But she was a little star, you know. She only made a little light. So the wind, it asked, 'Who will make more light?' The moon, she said she would make more light. The moon, she said she would make more light so all her children could see. But the wind, it complained this world was still too dark. 'Who will make further light?' it asked. The sun, she stood up in the east. The sun, she stood up in the east and said, 'I will shine my light everywhere. I will shine my light everywhere so everyone can see.' But as the sun, she stood up to bring light in the east she got a scratch from this world. This scratch, it made a drop of the sun's blood fall on this world. This drop of the sun's blood, it made the first Tsoyaha. This is why Tsoyaha are red. We are red because we are children of the sun. When the sun, she rises in the east and sets in the west she is red. This is the sun's scratch from this world. This scratch, it reminds us we are her children, you know."

With that Charles spat on the fire, ending his story.


## TURTLE ISLAND

One morning late in the summer of 2004 Charles and I walked the mountain in search of medicinal plants as we often now did. It was cool, and heavy dew sparkled on the plants as the orange-red sky yellowed and brightened. We spent an hour or so collecting plants before taking a break to sit on a log at the edge of his small algae covered pond. The sun rising in the sky was streaming beams of light through the trees. As the air warmed, insects scooted across the muddy green surface of the water. Charles touched my elbow and pointed. There was a turtle climbing onto a rock in the middle of the pond. As he lowered his arm and relaxed, he got that far away look and began to share a story.

"In the beginning this world was water, you know. This world, it was water and air. Life on this world were things of the water that swam and things of the air that could fly. They didn't need the land, you know. In the world above, up there in the sky world," he gestured with his chin and a sweeping motion of his arm, "there were many different peoples, plants, and animals. In the world below, this world, there was nothing." Tapping the ground with his foot. "There was nothing in the world below. It was a world of darkness. It was empty, you know. A great tree connected the three worlds. It was a great tree with many branches. Maybe it was a fruit tree, I don't know. But this tree, it was sacred to the sky people. Great father, he told the sky people to respect this tree and leave it alone.

"One of the sky women in the world above was with child. She wanted to see this sacred tree. When she sees this tree, she does not believe this tree is sacred. She tells her brother that this great tree is ugly.

She tells her brother to pull it up. When her brother, he pulls the great tree up, there was a large hole. It was a hole to the worlds below. Sky Woman, she goes to the edge of the hole to look at this world and the world below. Sky Woman, she goes to the edge of the hole and falls in, you know. She falls in and grabs at the dirt and grabs a fruit." Charles raises his arms as though he's falling and trying to grab something. "She falls a long way into this world. The birds of this world, they catch her with their wings and they put her on the back of a great sea turtle. They catch her, and they put her on the back of a sea turtle, and she is okay. The creatures of the great water, the crawfish, the toad, and the muskrat work together to make the land so that Sky Woman has a place to live. They work together and bring mud to put on the turtle's back. They put mud on the turtle's back, and the land began to grow.

"Pretty soon Sky Woman, she has her child. She has her child, and it was a daughter. Sky Woman's daughter, she grew fast. She grew fast and married the west wind. Pretty soon the daughter of Sky Woman, she is with child. The daughter of Sky Woman, she is with child and has a big belly. In her big belly the daughter of Sky Woman, she has twins. The first twin was born in the usual way. He was born in the usual way, and he was called Right Twin. The second twin was not born in the usual way. The second twin, he was born backward, you know, and the daughter of Sky Woman died because of it. The second twin, he was called Left Twin. Sky Woman, she placed the dirt and seeds from the fruit of the Sky World on her daughter's grave. From these seeds sacred plants, you know, like tobacco and sweetgrass and medicines, began to grow.

"These twins, they have special powers. They have special powers, and they can make things. Right Twin, he is gentle and emotional like a woman. He makes rolling hills, calm weather, flowers, and butterflies. Right Twin, he likes peace. Left Twin, he's not like Right Twin. Left Twin, he is rough and likes to think and plan like a man. He makes mountains, storms, thorny things, and things that bite like snakes, you know. Left Twin, he likes to fight. When Sky Woman, she dies, the twins, they fight over her body. They fight over her body, and they tear it to pieces. They fight over her body and throw her head into the sky." Charles gestures toward the sky with a sweeping motion of his right hand as though throwing a ball into the air. "They throw her head into the sky where it stayed. Her head, it stays up in the sky as Grandmother Moon. But these twins, they couldn't live together. They are all the time fighting. They couldn't live together fighting all the time, you know. They agreed to honor their mother. They agreed to live away from each other. They agreed to live away from each other to honor and show respect for Sky Woman, their grandmother. Right Twin, he chose to live in the light where he rules the day. Left Twin, he chose to live in the darkness and governs the night. In this way they honor and show respect for their grandmother."

Charles then spat and got up, indicating his story and our break were over.

## GRANDMOTHER SPIDER'S OVEN

On a hot summer afternoon Charles and I were walking the mountain. Even in the shade it was hot, and we were sweating. There was a nice thick log next to our trail and we decided to sit on it to take a break.

"Maybe there is something bad under this log. Maybe something can bite us. We should look under it," Charles suggested. So, we wedged our walking sticks under the log and rolled it over.

"Look there," he said pointing at a *very large* fishing spider. "I think maybe this could be Grandmother Spider. Oh, there's another spider," this time pointing at a black widow crouched in its mass of sticky web. "Maybe Grandmother Spider is baking. Maybe we shouldn't bother her," Charles continued. There were several other spiders, millipedes, sow bugs, and ants all hiding beneath the cool damp rotting log. "Maybe we should find another log to sit on." We rolled the log back over and continued up the trail until we found another log. There were only worms, beetles, and a salamander under this log, so we sat and rested on it.

"Why do you think that fishing spider back there was Grandmother Spider baking?" I asked out of curiosity.

"Because she is very large and very old, you know. Did you see her white hair and cloudy eyes? She likes to bake. But when she was a young girl, she did not bake very good, you know. One day when she was a girl she decided she was going to bake some people. The first batch, she baked them too long. They were hard and black. The next batch, she takes them out too soon. These people, they're not cooked. They were pale and soft. When she bakes her third batch, she watches them close, you know. These people, she baked them just right. They were brown and good. This is how Grandmother Spider, she makes the races of men."

Then he spat, stomped his walking stick on the ground, and got up.

## THE GIFT OF THE CORN

It was a warm summer afternoon about the first of August. There hadn't been much rain that summer. The forest was dry and thirsty, evidenced by its drooping leaves. The slow drive up the dirt road to Raven Ridge left a brownish plume of dust behind my white Ford Explorer as crushed limestone crunched under its tires. Parking in front of a log at Charles's workshop, I got out and went to the door. It was locked, and the lights in his shop were out, but his truck was parked nearby, so I knew he was around somewhere.

"Over here," I heard him call. As I looked, Charles was standing at the edge of the corn at his garden beckoning to me.

"I'm working in the garden today," he said. "I am glad you have come. The corn is almost ready. In a few days we celebrate the green corn. We have much work to do." I walked over to the garden and joined Charles by the corn. "The corn it is almost ripe. It's almost ready to harvest. See," he said, as he pulled the husk from the top of an ear of corn, separating its silky threads to expose small well-formed kernels. "We must make ready to receive the corn's gift. We must prepare ourselves and an area to receive it. We must fast and clean the area to give thanks and celebrate. This is good! You will help me!" he continued. Whatever it was we were about to do was important, and Charles was excited about it, not giving me any option but to pitch in and help for the next few days.

After inspecting a few more ears of corn, pulling a few weeds, and collecting some ripe veggies that we placed in a basket and took to his apartment, we moseyed down the mountain to a flat area Charles had begun to prepare earlier. In the center of the area was a fire ring. The large circle of dirt surrounding the fire ring was relatively clear of debris, but there were rocks, sticks, and leaves that had yet to be removed. Once that was accomplished we built four teepee-shaped brush piles at the four cardinal points of the circle marking north, east, south, and west, thus squaring the circle, and swept it clean with cedar boughs. This took us the better part of two days. We worked hard, hadn't eaten, and I was tired and starved! Our work wasn't done though. We had yet to harvest corn and consecrate the sacred area.

On the morning of the third day we harvested two bushels of corn. Charles said we had to pick out four perfect ears of corn from our harvest. This was easier said than done! When Charles was satisfied that the ears of corn selected were "perfect" we took them with great ceremony to the squared circle we had created and placed them next to the fire ring. Charles then lit a smudge he had made of cedar, white sage, tobacco, and sweetgrass bound by red and white threads, circumambulated the circle to purify the area with its dense smoke, chanting as he went.

That afternoon we played stickball, which was something like playing hockey with a stick and small ball. As the sun began to go behind the trees, Charles lit a large fire in the fire ring, then, one by one, the teepee-shaped brush piles beginning in the east and going clockwise to the north. He cast some tobacco into the air and began to chant and perform a stomp dance around the fire. After circling the fire a few times he motioned for me to join him. An hour or so later, exhausted, we sat down on a log near the fire and roasted our four perfect ears of corn. When Charles thought they were ready we pulled the roasted corn from the fire, peeled back the charred husks, and ate the fresh hot corn, savoring every bite. I swear to God I'd never been so hungry, and it was the best damn corn I'd ever eaten! Gawd it was soooo good!

As we sat in the firelight of the descending darkness smoking rolled tobacco, sending thanks and prayers on its smoke up to Great Father, Charles asked if I knew why the corn tasted so good.

"No", I said, taking a puff of sacred tobacco. "Maybe it's the kind of corn you grow." I exhaled. "Or maybe it's because I haven't eaten in three days. I don't know, but it's delicious!"

Leaning forward slightly, Charles gave me a sideways look. With a knowing grin he softly exhaled a breath of smoke, took a sip of snake-root tea, and solemnly said: "The corn, it is a gift. The corn, it is a blessing, you know." Gesturing at the fire: "This fire, it is sacred. This fire, it is part of the first fire. This fire, it is a blessing from our Great Father." Simultaneously pointing and looking up at the emerging stars. "This corn, this corn, it is a blessing from our Earth Mother," tapping the ground with his right foot. "When we roast the corn in the fire, when we roast the corn and eat we it after we fast to become pure, the corn it makes us feel good. It makes us thankful for something to eat, you know. We are not hungry. This roasted corn, it is blessed. It is blessed by the fire from Great Father when he comes together with the blessing of our Earth Mother. These blessings they come into us. These blessings they come into us when we eat the corn. It is because the corn is blessed in this way that it tastes so good, you know. The corn, it tastes good because we receive the blessings of Great Father and Earth Mother from it."

For a while we sat on the log in contemplative silence, occasionally poking at coals in the fire or gazing up at the stars, thinking about the green corn and its blessings. Charles faintly began humming, or perhaps he was chanting, I couldn't tell. Then, in a faraway whisper, he began sharing one of his stories:

"My teacher was an old man, you know. My teacher was an old

man. I was young when he first told me about the corn. He told me there was a time long ago when we didn't have corn. He told me there was a time before we had corn when the man was hungry. There was a man, he was hungry and looking for food, you know. The man, he was hungry and he looked for food on the mountain. There was no food on the mountain, so the man he went down to a field near a river. He went to this field near a river, and he heard a baby crying. At first he thought maybe the baby crying was a rabbit, a rabbit that was hurt, you know. He thought maybe the rabbit was hurt, and he could catch it and have some food, you know. So the man, he looks for where the rabbit is hiding. But the closer the man comes to the crying, the more it sounds like a baby and not a rabbit. The man is worried that a baby is lost in the field, and he looks for it. The man, he follows the sound of a baby crying to some bushes. He follows the sound of a baby crying to some bushes, and he finds a baby stalk of corn. The man, he finds a baby stalk of corn crying in the bushes near the river. The baby stalk of corn is crying and asks for the man's help. The baby stalk of corn is crying and asks the man to clear away the weeds so he can see the Sun. He asks the man to feed him and to get him a drink of water. The baby stalk of corn, he asks the man to take care of him. The man, he takes care of the baby stalk of corn. The man, he clears the weeds from near the baby stalk of corn so he can see the Sun. The man, he feeds the baby stalk of corn and brings him water. The man, he helps the baby stalk of corn so he can grow tall. When the corn, he grows tall he tells the man: 'I'm here to help you. I'm here to help all of your people. As long as you remember and never forget to help me you will not be hungry.'

"My teacher, he also told a story of an ugly old woman. She was an ugly old woman with sores all over her. She had sores all over her, and the people they were afraid, you know. The ugly old woman would scratch her sores or wipe her feet in the grass, and the corn, it would fall off of her. The people were afraid of her, but they helped her. They helped her because it was the right thing to do, you know. They helped her, and she gave them corn to eat. I wonder if the baby stalk of corn was her child. Maybe the baby stalk of corn was the ugly old woman's child, and he got lost. I don't know. But as long as we help the corn we are not hungry. The corn, that he grows tall, is a blessing from the Sun. That the corn, he feeds us so that we are not hungry is a blessing from Earth Mother. This is why corn is important you know. The corn it is a gift, and we must take care of it."

## HARMONY

Charles taught me about harmony. Among Native Americans corn, beans, and squash are known as the three sisters. This is because they are planted together. In modern terms we refer to this as co-planting. The three sisters harmonize with one another. Corn grows fast, tall, and strong. Corn stalks provide support and a place for beans to climb as they too reach for the sun. Beans replenish nitrogen in the soil that is needed and used by the corn. Squash grows on the ground at the feet of the corn and beans. It helps minimize weeds with its large leaves shading the feet of the corn and beans. Squash helps the roots of the corn and beans stay cool and retain water when it's hot. Planting these crops together also reduces the amount of area, the footprint, needed to produce a larger yield of these crops. If you think about it, our body, mind, and spirit work together like the three sisters.

## LEAVES OF GRASS

Not long after the green corn ceremony I made another trek up the mountain to visit Charles. I found him harvesting tobacco with a hand sickle near his garden. He grew traditional Native American tobacco (*Nicotiana rustica*) and had prepared his seedbeds in late winter, transplanting the seedlings in April shortly before we first met. During one of our early meetings he gifted me a few plants that I transplanted into my own garden. Now it was time to harvest and cure it. As Charles walked over to greet me he laid his sickle on a rocking chair on the small porch in front of his shop. Collecting his walking stick standing by the door he said, "Let's go check on my mushrooms and medicinal plants."

I retrieved my walking stick from the back of my Explorer, and we started down his steep drive to where a path split off to the left into the woods. It was a hot afternoon and the shade of the dappled forest was a cool respite. After nearly half a mile we arrived at an area cleared of underbrush that had logs stacked in the form of several four-sided pyramids about four-feet high. There were shiitake and oyster mushrooms growing on the logs. After inspecting the area for critter damage, we harvested some of the mushrooms, and Charles carefully placed them in a sack hanging by his side. Continuing down the trail a little ways was a small, cultivated plot facing the northwest that had plants in it. Many of the plants had their tops eaten off. It was evident from the disturbed leaves and tracks that deer had been dining on the ginseng and goldenseal Charles had planted. Only a few plants remained untouched, some with red berries. Charles was not happy!

"The plants the deer have eaten, they will not come back. They will die. We must dig the roots of these plants and put the berries under the leaves and mix them with the soil. The roots, they will be small. The roots, they have the medicine. It won't be much, but it will be enough. The seeds, they will make new plants in the spring. The new plants, they will take years to make roots big enough to make the medicine. Maybe the deer will be kind and let us have some. The deer, they are not greedy. Maybe the deer, they take what they need and leave us enough. This is nature's way, you know. Nature, she is about balance. Nature, she shares with everyone, you know. Maybe with Nature we don't get what we want. Maybe with Nature if we work in harmony with her, she gives us what we need. We must be content with that, you know."

Not taking the path, we trudged back up the steep mountain through the rock-strewn forest. Always on the lookout for medicinal plants and herbs, Charles, with his now bulging sack, spied some plants with tiny white wooly flowers in a moist sandy area by some boulders.

"Ah" he smiled, "I was hoping we would find this flower. Do you know this flower?" he asked stooping down to look at it.

Squatting next to him to get a better look at it I replied, "I know its name. It's called rabbit tobacco."

"Yes. Rabbit tobacco. It has good medicine. Maybe it looks like a small tobacco plant, but it's not tobacco. It grows in places like this late in summer. It has many uses, you know."

We collected a few plants that Charles carefully added to his sack.

"Maybe this is a good place to rest. I'm tired. Maybe we rest here for a little bit." With that Charles sat with his legs stretched out, his back against a tree, and hands behind his head.

"I'm thinking about tobacco," he began almost dreamily. "It's time to harvest the tobacco, you know. I think about my teacher. When he died, I gave him tobacco. I gave him tobacco as a gift for his ancestors. A gift so his ancestors would know him. A gift so he could be with his ancestors. My teacher, he was old. My teacher, he lived a good life. It was a great honor to do this for him, you know, to help him on his journey. I helped him on his journey to be something better. Maybe he's something better than when I knew him. Maybe he is like a butterfly. Maybe he is like that butterfly over there," gesturing toward a brown wood satyr flitting through the woods. Shifting to look at me, he asked: "Do you know the story of tobacco?" I admitted that I didn't know it, so he proceeded to tell me.

"A long time ago a man and a woman went into the woods. They went into the woods to a place like this. In a place like this they went to make love, and the man's semen, it falls on the ground. After they make love, the man and the woman, they go separate ways. They go separate ways after they make love. Later, the woman she comes back. The woman, she comes back, and she finds this strange plant. She finds this strange plant where the man's semen fell on the ground when they made love. The woman thinks the plant is beautiful. The woman, she finds the man and shows him the beautiful plant. The man and the woman do not know this plant, you know. The man and the woman don't have a name for this plant. The woman, she has a son. She has a son and takes him to see the plant. The woman asks her son what is the plant. The boy, he studies the plant. The boy, he learns the plant is good medicine. The boy, he learns that smoke from the plant carries prayers to Great Father. The boy, he tells the woman 'I will name this plant. I will name this plant tobacco.'"

## UP IN SMOKE

By September of 2004, I had been visiting with Charles several times a week for six months. Regardless of what he was doing Charles made time for me. When I visited he would take up his hiking stick and say, "let's go for a walk." Off we would go tromping the mountain to find plants and talk.

Back in the spring he inspired me to grow an herb garden of sweet-grass, sage, and tobacco. He said: "These are important plants, you know. They are from Earth Mother. These plants, they give up their lives, so we can have their smoke. These plants, they give up their lives so that we can send our prayers up to Great Father on their smoke. This smoke, it helps us look inside. It helps us remember. This smoke, it makes us awake and helps us remember. It helps us remember when we are lost."

When I harvested, cured, and dried my few plants of tobacco, I wrapped some of it in a piece of red cloth bound by a string tied in knots. I took this bundle to Charles and kept it in my pocket, waiting for the right time to present it to him. While we were squatted down discussing the red berries of a ginseng plant, I pulled the tobacco from my pocket and presented it to him. He took the little red package, gave me a sideways look, and grinned as he stood up.

"What is this?" he asked.

"It's a gift. Do you accept it?" I asked.

"This is a fine gift. Let me think about it. Let's walk for a while and maybe I will know."

With that Charles placed the tobacco in his left shirt pocket. He tried hard to be serious but was all smiles as we walked farther into the woods.

As we walked Charles casually pointed out some plants, asked me what they were used for, and how to find them. While we sat on a log taking a break, a spider with an egg sac ran from the leaves under the log. Charles asked if I remembered the story about Grandmother Spider's oven. I did, so he asked me to tell him the story. "Hmmm," he said, after I repeated the story as close to how he told it as I could. As we walked some more, Charles asked more questions about plants and their uses. He asked me to relate the story about the game between the birds and animals. He wanted to know what I thought it meant and what its lesson was.

We stopped at a spring for a drink of cool mountain water. Lying down to get a drink Charles asked if I saw anything in the water.

"No. Am I supposed to see something?" I asked.

Charles said: "I don't know. Maybe. There's a little white flower. Maybe you can see the little white flower."

I looked again in the water. Still I didn't see anything. "There are many white flowers. Does this white flower have a name?" I asked.

"It does," said Charles grinning. "This flower, its name is white snakeroot. Ask the water to show you where is this flower. Be still in your mind. Be respectful in your heart. Be patient. Maybe she will show you."

I lay on the ground for a long time looking into the water. Over and over in my mind I asked the water to show me where I could find white snakeroot. Watching the ripples and swirls of the spring's trickling water was mesmerizing. I became so entranced that I wanted to close my eyes and go to sleep right where I lay. It was then that I began to see something in the water through half-closed eyes! It was clusters of tiny white flowers glimmering like a reflection! Its dark green leaves were broad and veiny. It was growing in a moist partially shaded area that I sensed was nearby.

"Charles," I said slowly turning my head, "I see the white snakeroot flower. I think it's close by. Over there," pointing to my left and some-what in front of me while still on my belly. "Let's go find this flower."

I got up, brushed the leaves and dirt from my shirt, stretched, took a few breaths, and closed my eyes. In my mind I could still see the lit-tle white flower clusters and broad green leaves of the snakeroot. As I turned my body I sensed the direction it was in. With a picture of it in my mind I began walking in the direction I felt the flower was grow-ing. Charles followed without a sound. We walked a little more than a hundred yards through the woods. I sensed that the flower was close. It was a very strong feeling. I paused and began looking around for it. Scanning the area, I looked for a partially shaded damp area. Not see-ing one I advanced a few more yards and noticed a slightly rounded drop-off trending downhill. Dappled sunlight illuminated the silvery gray trunk of a young beech tree just below the drop-off. There it was! There was a small clump of white snakeroot near the base of a beech tree. Jumping up and down with excitement I shouted "I found it! I found the flower!" With a big ear-to-ear smile Charles patted me on the back. Then he put his hand on my shoulder and looked me square in the eye. "I'm happy you found this flower," is all he said.

In barely contained excited silence we walked the well-trodden path back to Charles's gravel driveway and on up the mountain. When we arrived at his lodge, Charles collected a few cedar branches and started a small fire in the stone fire pit. On a thick log near the fire we sat together in contemplative silence. We watched the crackling fire spit sparks that drifted lazily upward to disappear on its smoke. After a while Charles spoke:

"I've been thinking about your gift. I think it is a great honor to accept such a fine gift, you know," he said patting the packet of tobacco in the pocket over his heart. "It's good we sit together like this you know, as brothers. Tomorrow the seasons, they change, you know. Tomorrow is important. The hours of the day and the hours of the night, they are the same. When it's not light and not dark the lower world and the upper world can sit together and talk. It's important because you will learn to be awake. You will learn to remember. We will sing your song tomorrow and remember this day. We will remember the corn and ask for her blessings. We will send prayers to Great Father on the smoke. We have work to do."

With that Charles stood up and added more cedar branches to the fire along with a little sweetgrass. Bright orange-yellow flames burst forth and danced as the fire snapped, crackled, and popped, sending up a fresh plume of spiraling smoke and sparks. A faint smell of cedar mixed with sweetgrass began to fill the air.

For the remainder of the day we cleaned and purified the area around the lodge, occasionally adding more cedar and sweetgrass to the fire. We began by cleaning the inside of the lodge, sweeping down debris and spider webs from its top to its floor. We removed the old, dried cedar branch bedding. Rocks in the fire pit were cleaned and repositioned. After every corner of the floor was swept with homemade brooms and debris was removed, we added fresh cedar branches having soft green needles. Charles used smoke from a smoldering sage smudge to purify the inside of the lodge. He then lit a small cedar wood fire in its pit, adding sweetgrass to it. Outside we removed small rocks, twigs, and leaves from inside the stone circle surrounding the lodge, sweeping it clean. Again, Charles used smoke from a smoldering sage smudge to purify the area.

It was beginning to get dark, and I hadn't eaten all day. Excitement from the day's events and all the cleaning made me hungry and tired, but Charles said we must not eat. As darkness fell we began to play a game of football. Illuminated by flickering firelight, tree shadows danced around us. The intoxicating fragrance of cedar and sweetgrass filled the air and my lungs as we ran back and forth playing our game of one-on-one. It wasn't until the wee morning hours that we stopped. Charles stood at the edge of the circle away from the fire and thoughtfully gazed up at the stars.

"It's time for us to go in. We will sit together and talk. Soon you will be awake, you know. Soon you will remember."

We walked over to the lodge, pulled back its blue tarp door, and went in.

The faint glow of burning red embers was all I could see in the darkness. It was warm, almost hot, inside. As Charles added a few twigs of green-needled red cedar to the glowing embers they burst into smoky flame. Smoke curled and swirled as it rose to find its way out of a round hole in the roof. We sat and talked together of many things in the dancing glow of the little fire. Occasionally Charles added a few more green cedar twigs along with tobacco to the fire, causing it to smoke. The combination of cedar and tobacco smoke made me feel funny. I was somewhat high from it and was beginning to sweat. At some point Charles produced a short-stemmed pipe carefully wrapped in white cloth. Its engraved decoration was worn almost smooth as was its blackened stone bowl. It looked to be very old. Removing a small brown leather pouch from around his neck Charles placed some of its contents in the small pipe bowl, tamped it lightly, and lit it. As he exhaled a puff of smoke he said: "You do not know this plant. It's an important plant. It's a sacred plant. It will make you awake. It will help you remember. It's time for the lower world to sit and talk with the upper world. Smoke this pipe with me." With great reverence he extended the pipe with both hands. I accepted.

I accepted the pipe with both hands, took an apprehensive puff, exhaled as Charles had done, and handed it back to him. He took another puff, exhaled, bowed his head and whispered: "I think maybe I'm the last one. Maybe I'm the last of what First Peoples they call 'Old Ones,' the Anikutani, you know. I think maybe there are no more of us."

He passed the pipe to me, I took a puff and handed it back. Charles took another puff, continuing: "My teacher, he died many years ago. He was old. He had a good life, you know. He said he didn't know any old ones. He only knew his teacher. A long time ago we were important to all First Peoples. We helped them. We were respected. The white man he came and brought his priests. These priests, they didn't like us. They told the people we were bad. They told the people we were a poison, you know." Passing the pipe to me, he went on: "The people they became afraid. They became afraid, so they hunted and killed us. Some of us, we ran away. We ran away to the mountains. The people, they didn't find all of us. Some of us, we lived, you know." I took a deep draw on the pipe, exhaled, and passed it back to Charles who had cocked his head looking at me. "Some of us, we lived but we changed so the people they wouldn't know us."

Everything went black, pitch black! I couldn't see anything. I couldn't hear anything. I couldn't smell or feel anything. Timeless impenetrable blackness is all there was. Ever so slowly I began to sense that I was floating in this eternal blackness. There was a faint coarse raspy kind of sound emerging from somewhere. It was growing louder. What was it? I felt air movement and something soft brush past my face. What was that? It was becoming light now. There was a soft reddish-orange glow diffused by white fog. I seemed to be in a cedar tree atop a mountain, Charles's mountain. It was sunrise.

On a branch sitting next to me was a raven. It was hopping up and down shaking the branch and cawing. What the heck? The raven cocked its head looking at me and cawed again. Then it hopped off the branch into the air and flew, circling the cedar tree a few times. Returning to the branch next to me it bobbed its head up and down and cawed some more. Again, the raven cocked its head, looked at me, cawed, and flew around the tree. Was it trying to tell me something? Did it want me to follow it? The raven perched next to me yet again, performing its head bobs and cawing. This time when it dropped out of the tree to fly I decided to follow it. *Oh my God! I was flying!* We circled the tree and landed on another branch. What a rush! We took off again and flew a little farther before returning. Several times we did this, flying a little farther, a little longer each time. I was getting the hang of it now.

We leapt from the cedar tree, flying toward the diffused orange sunrise, soaring over wispy fog rising from the mountain, hollows, and rivers. Words fail to capture the sensation and beauty of it all! For the remainder of the day we flew. We flew to many places, landing here and there to look at things. The moon rose, and the sun became a glowing orange orb again. It was a long exhilarating day! I was tired and needed rest. I needed to sleep. We flew back to the cedar tree atop the mountain where we began. Perched on a limb looking out over the mountain the world was far below us. We could see everything. We were part of everything and everything was part of us. We were one with the world!

It was growing dark. Memories began flooding my mind with the force of a tsunami. Memories of things I'd buried deep long ago and forgotten. Memories of people, places, and events from long before I was born flash-flooded my mind as a burst of brilliant white light. I was wide awake, and I knew. I was awake, and I remembered! With a loud crack the light was gone. I was floating in silent blackness. Floating. Then there was nothing.

My whole body ached. My head hurt. My hair hurt. My eyeballs hurt. Everything hurt. Slowly I squinted open my crusty eyes and turned my head. Rays of smoke-filtered sunlight streamed in from the vent hole in the roof of the lodge. Curled in a fetal position on soft green cedar branches I lay hurting. Little by little I moved and stretched until I could sit up. I felt worse than if I'd been out on an all-night drunk and woken up with a horrible hangover. My mind was in a dense fog. Gosh, I felt rough!

Finally, I managed to sit and shake my head, trying to loosen the cobwebs from my mind. Charles was sitting next to me, quiet without expression, keenly watching with those blue wolf eyes.

"Can you stand up?" he asked, helping me to my feet. "Let's go outside. Maybe the fresh air it will help you." With his arm around me he helped me stumble through the door of the lodge over to the log by the fire pit where I plopped down. Handing me a wooden bowl he said, "Drink this tea. It will help you feel better. It will give you strength."

Sitting hunched over on the log I sipped the tea and jerked upright, coughing and spitting, "Good grief, Charles! What's in this tea? This is nasty!"

Charles laughed. "Ha ha ha! Maybe this tea it doesn't taste good. Maybe you hold your nose like this," he said, pinching his nose. "You must drink all this tea. Soon you will feel better."

Reluctantly I pinched my nose and drank my tea until the bowl was empty.

"Maybe you can stand up now. Maybe walk a little bit." I took a few deep breaths to clear my lungs, stretched, stood up, and walked around the perimeter of the lodge. My foggy mind was beginning to clear and I was feeling better, not hurting quite so bad. Returning to the log to sit next to Charles I remembered what happened the night before.

"How long was I out? What time is it? What day is it?" I asked cluelessly.

"Maybe you sleep a few hours. It's morning. Maybe you can tell me about last night?" He wryly queried with a grin.

So, I shared my experiences with the raven, flying, memories, the bright light, and the darkness. Charles listened intently to every word without expression. When I finished he smiled big and slapped his knee.

"Now you are awake. Now you remember. You are changed. I am happy that we sit together and talk as brothers. We must thank the corn and ask her blessings. We must send prayers to Great Father on the smoke and sing. First we rest."

Lying on soft green cedar boughs we slept until midafternoon within the stone circle surrounding the lodge and fire pit. When we got up, the cedar branches we slept on were placed in the fire and burned. I cleaned and swept the area, purifying it with a sage smudge. Charles made medicinal tea. As afternoon turned to dusk we roasted four fresh ears of corn. We thanked the corn for her sacrifice, asking her continued blessings. Remembering the corn, we drank our tea and gave thanks. It was the first I'd eaten in almost three days. I was hungry and thankful. I was blessed!

As darkness fell, countless stars peered down from the heavens above. We made our fire big. Cedar boughs snapped and popped as they burned, spewing star-like sparks that rose to greet the heavens on fragrant thick smoke. Tree shadows danced to the rhythm of flickering flames. In the firelight amid the smoke and sparks we joined the shadows of our ancestors in their flame dance. Sending prayers up to Great Father, we celebrated and sang late into the night as the three worlds sat together and talked as one.

## TRANSMUTATION

The summer of 2005 was hot! How many days were in the nineties or above I don't know. But it was hot and continued through September. I had been visiting Charles, walking the mountain with him, and learning from him for about a year and a half. Charles had taught me about plants, about the nature of things, about the universe, about life. He imparted knowledge and shared stories that taught lessons. He taught me the old ways, the lost ways of the Anikutani—ways of thinking and doing that changed my perceptions and worldview. I thought I knew a lot back then. But as Charles said when we first met, I still had much to learn. During the fall equinox of that year I endured a most humbling learning experience, an experience that would forever change me.

The fall equinox was approaching, the three worlds would sit together and talk. It's an important mysterious time. It was a year since I was introduced to the smoke and had my first out-of-body experience, learning how to see, learning how to change. In that year I advanced in knowledge and ability. It was time for another lesson! So, it was on a hot late summer day, the morning of September 22 in 2005, that Charles informed me we were taking a little trip. Grinning, he said it was going to be more like an adventure. Excited, yet apprehensive, I helped him load our two small packs of food and water and our hiking sticks, tossing them into the bed of an old truck.

"Where are we going?" I asked.

He replied, "Oh, did I not tell you? My friend, he is driving us to the other end of the mountain. We are going to see the equinox. You and me, we walk back on the mountain."

With that the three of us piled into his friend's truck. Down the mountain we bounced leaving a thick cloud of dust behind us. An hour or so later we drove up the steep winding gravel road of switchbacks at the other end of the mountain, parked, and got out at a trailhead.

As Charles's friend drove off, we shouldered our packs and took up our hiking sticks. It was almost noon and already hot when we set off on the trail. Crossing a large gray slab of limestone next to a cedar tree we entered the shaded, cooler mixed forest of dappled sunlight. The trail was steep as it climbed a ridge for the first half a mile before leveling off. There was a side trail on our left leading to a small clearing offering a tree-framed overlook of the valley below. We took a break, had a drink of water, and enjoyed the view. Returning to the main trail, it wound and undulated for another half mile to a fork. We went left on a smaller trail that soon passed a large limestone boulder field. Navigating gaps between the boulders was treacherous and led to a dense thicket of rhododendron. Emerging from an opening in the thicket we stepped out on a cliff. It was spectacular!

Standing on fossil-encrusted rock we were 2,000 feet above the valley floor, 4,000 feet up. There was an unobstructed 220-degree view of the horizon in the west. To the left was a natural gap in the mountain. Like a serpent's tail, the mountain snaked southwest until it faded in the hazy distance. A patchwork of farm fields spread out below for as far as the eye could see. Birds sang, buzzards circled, and ravens flew below us. A pair of falcons zipped past with a whoosh as they plummeted from the cloudless sky above. Breathtaking!

We stood there in wonder and awe a long time just taking it all in, enjoying the moment for what it was. Finally, Charles said we had work to do. We collected rocks, made a fire ring, gathered wood, lit a small fire, established a protective circle, and purified the area. After exploring and gathering some plants, we roasted a few ears of corn. As we ate in contemplative silence, Charles gazed westward. It was late in the afternoon, moving toward evening. The sun was lower in the sky. Charles broke our silence pointing at the sun.

"It is time for the equinox. Soon the three worlds will sit here together to talk. My people, they came to this place. They call this place Buzzard Rock now. They came to this place called Buzzard Rock on this day for a long time. We must make the fire bigger and sing. We must pray to Great Father. We must do this so the three worlds, they can talk. We must do this so my ancestor's spirits, they protect us in our journey tonight."

As we added wood to the fire its flames grew. Thick smoke, fragrant with green cedar, bellowed and curled upward as the fire crackled and spit sparks high into the reddening sky. Placing slashes of red paint on our faces we danced with the shadows and sang prayers to Great Father. We let the fire burn down and put it out when it became dark and Venus set in the west.

When the fire was completely out we cleaned the area, leaving it as though we were never there.

"It is time," Charles said. "It is time for us to begin our journey to the east."

Charles placed his hands firmly upon my shoulders and turned me to face him. Even in the blackness I felt his piercing blue wolf eyes upon me. In a hushed voice he warned: "I have told you this mountain, she is old, and she is wise. You must respect her, you know. You must be strong. Brave. Do not show fear. You must be prepared here," thumping my chest. "Maybe this mountain she tests you. Maybe this mountain she will share her secrets. When you are alone on this mountain, she will test you. When you are with me you are protected. Do you remember these things? Do you trust me?"

"Yes." I nervously replied.

"Tonight, the three worlds they sit together here on this mountain. Tonight, this mountain she will know you. Tonight, this mountain she will test you. She is dangerous! Do you understand? Are you ready? Do you take this journey?"

Again, I nervously responded that I was. Twice more he asked if I wanted to proceed. Twice more I replied in the affirmative.

He continued: "Tonight, we ask the spirits of my ancestors for protection. Maybe the spirits of my ancestors, they help you. Tonight, the mountain she is awake, you know. She protects the three worlds and will not be friendly. When we go to the east you walk in front. You must find this path. See this path in your mind. Stay on this path. Do not leave it! Stay strong. Be brave when something happens. Clear your mind. Find this path. When you see this path in your mind, follow it."

I took a few deep, cleansing breaths. Relaxed. Cleared my mind. In my mind's eye I saw a way off the cliff through the rhododendron thicket. A sudden gust of chilly west wind rose up out of the valley, causing me to shiver. There were goose bumps on my naked arms, and the hairs on the back of my neck stood up.

I took a deep breath. Knowing I had to trust my abilities, in inky darkness I hopped off a rock from the cliff into the rhododendron thicket. Even though it was so dark I literally couldn't see a hand in front of my face, in my mind's eye I saw an illuminated path. Charles was close behind as we dodged branches, stooped, and slowly navigated the thicket toward the boulder field. Crossing the boulder field was risky. I couldn't physically see the gaps and crevices between rocks in the darkness of the forest. I had to see them with my mind's eye.

We were creeping cautiously along and were about halfway across when something heavy and long slithered across my foot. *Shhh shhh shhh shhh shhh. Shhh shhh shhh shhh shhh. Shhh shhh shhh shhh shhh.* It sounded something like a baby's rattle. Oh shit! Timber rattler! I froze, calmed myself, relaxed, and didn't dare move a muscle. The sound of rattlers was all around us. We were in a den of rattlesnakes! During the heat of the day the snakes found coolness hiding under rocks and leafy debris in shaded crevices. At night they came out of hiding to warm themselves on top of the rocks and to hunt. This was not a good time to be crossing this boulder field! I had to center myself, think, and find a way out of this predicament.

Charles whispered firmly in the darkness behind me: "Don't move!" I heard him tapping and scraping his stick on the rocks to the left of me.

He was distracting the snake with vibration, causing it to slither away. I could hear him slide his pack off his shoulder and get something out. A fine dust descended as Charles tossed something into the night air and chanted. In a hushed voice he whispered, "Use your stick. Use your stick on the rocks. Move slow with heavy feet. I think maybe the snakes they will not bother us." The volume of rattles subsided, but every now and again one would alert nearby. We heard the snakes slither and slide across the leaves and rocks, dropping with a thud into the litter of cracks and crevices. Tapping rocks, slowly we advanced. Finally, we were across the snake-infested boulder field. It wasn't until we reached the fork in the path well beyond it that we rested. Flopping down on my back in the middle of the path my heart was pounding hard in my chest. *That* was a close call! Too close! One wrong move or bad decision and we both would have been bitten and killed!

Lying on our backs we calmed ourselves and rested. Once the adrenaline rush had passed I got on my feet, centered myself, and again sought the path with my mind. We moved off in the darkness of the forest along an undulating ridge to our left. My senses were now heightened. I was hypervigilant, sensitive to any noise, movement, or presence. For a long time our hike was uneventful. Occasionally deer would snort, stomp, or run through the woods. A raccoon up in a tree chattered at us. Nothing out of the ordinary. The night sky began to brighten, and we could see a little bit. Further on there was an opening in the trees on our right. The bright rising moon was about three-quarters full, and Mars was close to it. Both were reflected in the lake below. A gentle breeze from the southwest caused leaves to rustle and branches to sway. It was almost as though they were whispering.

A whiff of something pungent wafted faintly on the breeze. Nose in the air, my nostrils flared like a hound dog. The stench became stronger as we walked. Bear! Unmistakably a bear! Ahead in the moonlight I saw a tree that a bear had rubbed the bark off of. At its base was a large pile of fresh soft scat. As the wind was blowing from southwest to northeast we were upwind of the bear. He no doubt smelled us and was running the ridge ahead. In the dark distance it sounded like something heavy crashing through dense brush, making a lot of noise. It was the bear letting us know he was there. We responded in turn by banging our sticks on tree trunks and shaking the brush. Our sentiments were mutual. The bear didn't want an encounter with us anymore than we wanted one with him. The bear continued to make noise and thrash through forest undergrowth as it moved away from us down the north side of the ridge.

Again, I collected myself, saw the path in my mind's eye, and vigilantly continued east as before under the silvery light of the rising moon. We walked at a good pace for a very long time. When we reached a large open field we were sweaty, tired, and ready for a break. After a drink of water, I lay on my back and gazed up at the stars. Charles sat next to me. It was a clear night, the stars twinkled brightly, and we had an unobstructed view of the heavens. The moon was high in the sky in the south, and Mars was next to her. Cassiopeia was in the north. As I lay quietly in the field a meteor shot across the sky. A while later another flashed by, then another. Charles said the meteors were messengers of the three worlds.

It was a refreshing break, but we still had quite a ways to go and had to get moving. Back on the path we crossed the field and entered the forest again. Initially it was easy going, uneventful, and we made good time. Then it became steeper, rocky, and closed in as we trended downhill. The wind picked up and really began to blow. I didn't like it. Something wasn't right. I could feel it. Then the hair on the back of my neck stood up. Coyotes began to howl! There was a pack of them, barking and yipping, running toward us. They ran out of the brush and across the path immediately in front of us. Two adults and several younger ones. We continued for several yards when they darted out again behind us. Vigilantly we advanced. Ahead in the moonlight a solitary coyote stood in the path with its legs spread apart, head lowered, and growling, barring our way. Without thinking I instantly charged it with my arms raised like a bear, yelling, and swinging my stick. Startled by my response, the coyote tucked its tail and ran off yipping into the brush to join its pack that was howling behind us.

"That was brave. Foolish, but brave." Charles said patting me on the back. "You were not afraid?" he queried.

"I don't know. I didn't think about it. I just did what had to be done," I replied.

"I am happy that you are brave. The mountain, she knows this too," is all he said.

Continuing along the path it became rockier, winding its way steeply upward. The rocks were no longer limestone, rather sandstone. They were becoming larger, and patches of white sand glowed in the moonlight around the bases of what seemed to be formations over-arched by large rhododendrons. Up ahead in the distance loomed a shadowy beehive-shaped formation that seemed to shimmer. The path in my mind's eye led us to an entrance at its base. Entering it was like stepping into another world! It was a canyon-like crevice with tower-ing walls. The Moon peered in from high above, illuminating the path, causing the sandy white floor to glow. There was a soothing low buzz-ing noise that sounded almost like the humming of bees as the wind coursed through the crevices. I had this overwhelming feeling of being exhausted and sleepy. Without a care in the world I wanted to lie down right where I was and sleep. Charles grabbed me up by my elbow and admonished me to keep going. We would rest shortly he said.

Reluctantly I shuffled forward one foot at a time. It was as much a mental struggle as it was physical. I don't know how far we went into this crevice. Quite a ways I suppose. But I really don't know, as I was out of it. Eventually we arrived at a place that had two biscuit-shaped cuts in the rock, one above the other containing soft sand. Charles said we could rest here and helped me crawl into the upper cut. Immediately I was out like a light, embraced by dreams and visions. Things I won't talk about.

Charles was shaking me by my elbow. Slowly I opened my eyes. It was still dark, but the sky above was becoming light, and birds were singing as I slid off the sand-filled ledge. I felt refreshed but hungry after my little nap. Taking a drink of water, I was ready to continue. In the dawning light I could just make out Charles standing there grinning at me. All I could do was laugh and shake my head.

"Let's go," I said beckoning him. With that I sauntered off as though I knew exactly where we were going. Meandering through the crevices we eventually arrived at an exit. A Christmas fern, illuminated by the first light of day, was growing there in the sand.

Exiting the crevices, we were confronted by large, lush rhododendrons arching over the sandy path. After a short distance the path led to a slight embankment above the verdant shrubbery. We were on top of a knob. In its center was a large old cedar tree. Ravens were hopping up and down in it, cawing. The sky was changing from orange to yellow. I climbed the boulders bordering the knob and looked to the east. The first rays of the rising sun were just beginning to peek over a neighboring mountain. I was stunned! I couldn't believe it! This is where I was in my vision last year! This was the place where I changed into a raven and learned to fly! It was real! I was becoming emotional. All I could do was look at Charles in awe. He had that big ear-to-ear smile and was nodding his head up and down.

After sunrise, as I collected myself, we washed the red paint from our faces. Charles informed me that it was Sunday. We had been gone for three full nights.

"When the three worlds sat together on this mountain, this mountain, she looks into your heart. This mountain, she tested you. This mountain, she wants to know if you can sit with the three worlds. This mountain, she wants to know if you are Anikutani, you know. Down there," gesturing toward the crevices with his head, "you died. You go to the lower world," moving his open left hand in a downward motion. "You go to the upper world," pointing at the sky with his right index finger. "You come back to this world from the dead," he said with both hands open in front of him. "This mountain, now she shares her secrets with you. These things are between this mountain and you, you know.

We will paint our faces white to remember your death my brother. You are Anikutani now. Tonight, we celebrate. Tonight, we will eat the corn. We will make a big fire. It will have much smoke to send messages of thanks to Great Father. We will thank our ancestors. We will thank this mountain. Tonight, we will sing your song!"

## THE RAVEN

Late on a mild Saturday afternoon at the end of January in 2006 I drove the one-lane road of switchbacks up the mountain to visit Charles. It was several degrees colder on the mountaintop, and a brisk wind accentuated it. A few inches of crunchy snow speckled with bird and animal tracks and protruding plant heads covered the ground. Charles was on the phone in his shop when I pulled into the parking area in front. I had barely opened my car door when he came over with his stick and said: "I am happy you have come here today. It is a good day to go for a walk. Let's walk together in the forest. Tonight, we will sit together and talk by the fire."

We walked on the mountain until sunset identifying animal tracks in the snow, scat, and winter birds. There were several different animal tracks near Charles's lodge, mostly night visitors such as squirrel, raccoon, possum, fox, skunk, deer, coyote, and an occasional bobcat. By looking at their scat we determined that they were eating mice, chipmunks, squirrels, birds, scavenged carcasses, and stemmy plants and nuts. The winter birds were seedeaters who foraged their food from snow-covered plants, seeds left on trees, and pine cones.

Just before dark we huddled on a large log in front of a small crackling fire in front of his lodge. Draped with heavy wool blankets, we sipped hot sassafras tea. As the sky darkened stars began to appear one by one through wisps of swaying smoke. It was a crisp, clear night, and the heavens soon became star-spangled under a new moon.

For the longest time we sat in silence just gazing at the emerging stars. After a long while Charles gestured with his stick to Orion rising in the south. "In winter Great Father, he stands to watch over us. Sky Woman is there too," pointing at Cassiopia. Then pointing toward the northeast, "The Big Dipper, it stands tall in the sky. Soon it will be time to make the field ready for corn. When spring equinox, it comes, Great Father appears to die. But he does not die. He goes hunting with his twin (referring to Ophiuchus) in the world below. He comes back to life, he comes back to Sky World in August, you know."

Again, pointing with his stick: "There is the Milky Way. It is small now. The Milky Way it is the Great River of Sky World. This world it floats in the Great River. There are many worlds floating in the Great River, you know," he said looking directly at me making sure I understood what he was saying. "In summer when we see the Great River it is large and rises like a great smoke. In winter the Great River, when we see it, it is small like a stream. This world, it does not float in the middle of the Great River. This world it floats in a stream of the Great River. This world, it floats in a stream of the Great River with other worlds, you know," Charles said, still looking at me while adding wood to the fire causing it to spark and smoke. "But the Great River, it is not a river," he continued, cocking his head askance. "The Great River, it is smoke from the First Fire. The Great River, it is smoke from the First Fire that rises high into the Sky World. The smoke, it rises into the Sky World and goes in circles with the wind. This world and other worlds are sparks from the First Fire floating in the smoke. This world and other worlds float in circles in the smoke of the First Fire, you know." Charles now stood. In the soft yellow-orange glow of the fire, still gripping his stick, he raised and stretched his arms out to his sides, tilted his head back, and gazed up at the stars; allowing the burgeoning swirling smoke to envelop him as he related this. Then he began to chant.

Charles waned, "The Eagle he lives high in the Sky World near Great Father. He is strong, he is wise, and he is brave. The bat, he lives in the world below with the dead. He has strong medicine to make new life. The bat, he's a good listener and keeps secrets. The wolf, he lives in this world. He has strong magic. The wolf, he is wise and a good leader, but like the snake he gets confused. He protects this world, but he can destroy it. The raven, he is black because he flies in the smoke when he takes messages from the three worlds to Great Father. The Raven is crafty and a trickster."

You know Xas'i, in this smoke you cannot see clearly. This smoke, it plays tricks. This world, it is a spark in the smoke of the First Fire. This world, it goes in circles like a spark in the smoke. What we see in this world is not the same in other worlds."

Gesturing upward, he continued: "Everything is part of the Sky World, and the Sky World is part of everything. Great Father, he lives in the middle of the Sky World. Great Father, he doesn't know time or distance. Time and distance are for this world. Time and distance do not live in the Sky World. In the Sky World there is only the thought of Great Father. Great Father, he looks into the Great River. Great Father, he looks into the Great River, and it reflects his thoughts. Maybe when Great Father, he looks into the Great River, it reflects the sparks from the first fire. Maybe it reflects the spark of this world, and he sees two of this world and two of other worlds. I cannot explain this, you know."

Charles spat and we began to muse about other things.

## VISION QUEST

Charles was constantly sending me in search of something. Usually it was to find things I knew little or nothing about. He would ask me to go find something, you know, a plant maybe. But before I searched for it I had to find a spring, look into the water, meditate, and ask the spring where was this plant. I learned to draw upon the water.

Charles died in a terrible car accident in the fall of 2006. During one of my last visits with him on the mountain he looked at a photo I had just taken of a bird. After a moment's scrutiny he smiled and said: "You take pretty good pictures of birds now, you know. You have learned to capture their spirit. It's time you take pictures of other things." Handing the camera back to me he said: "Down the mountain over there is an orange flower. Its name is a Carolina lily. I think maybe she is still blooming. I am tired today and need to take my medicine. Go find me this flower and take a picture of her so I can see her."

I had no clue what a Carolina lily looked like but went in search of it as he asked. First, I fasted and purified myself. Next, I went to a spring near Charles's lodge. As I gazed meditatively into the rippled water of its small pool an orange flower appeared in a meadow. I knew what the flower looked like now and where to find it.

I began down Charles's broad dirt road, then picked up a well-worn path and followed it for a ways. The path branched off and narrowed into numerous smaller trails as I went. I passed the small pond with frogs and turtles sunning on a log in the water along its muddy bank. Birds sang in the leafy green trees above; insects hummed and buzzed. A wolf spider with babies clinging to her back scurried among fallen brown leaves. Plants I didn't recognize a few years ago were now familiar. As I pressed forward deeper into the forest the warm sunlight gave way to cool dappled shade. I weaved my way among ever narrowing and barely noticeable game trails. Then there was no path. I was in a place I hadn't been before surrounded by gnarly broken trees. A long black snake was draped over a fallen limb. I slowed and watched it glide off from the corner of my eye. Continuing in the direction it had gone I navigated dense thorny brush that ripped at my clothing and skin. I scrambled and slipped several times in the scree of a precipitously deep ravine and nearly fell climbing a cliff. A barred owl hooted. It was getting dark and I could barely see. As I came to a clearing in the forest I found the orange flower alone by a stream in a small meadow. It was still blooming. After studying it for a time, I photographed it. Returning to the top of the mountain I showed Charles my photo of the flower.

"I am happy you found this flower," is all he said. Then we sang.

# 11
# FINDING THE GRAIL

Many who dabble in the occult, in hidden things, often specialize in either Western occultism, Eastern mysticism, or some form of shamanism. For most of my life my knowledge and efforts centered on the occult. I did well, learned and grew, but I plateaued. Something was holding me back, preventing me from advancing. Something was missing that I couldn't identify.

I've always had an affinity for nature and the natural world, but those interests were kept separate from my occult and mystical ones. Classic occultism and mysticism appear to be a positive, left-brain, masculine function. In contrast, shamanism appears to be a negative, right-brain, feminine function. Our brain incorporates the principles of gender and polarity. It wasn't until Charles's death that I realized the necessity of navigating them, sailing a middle passage toward a hidden mystical third pillar, toward equilibrium, to find beauty in all things. It was the Dutch painter Vincent van Gogh, the one who cut off his ear, who said: "If you truly love nature, you will find beauty everywhere."

Meditation is the vehicle that enables us to navigate between the left- and right-brain pillars. It provides the grounding necessary for the unification of opposites that enhances awareness, efficiency, and effectiveness. It completes an electrical circuit that significantly accentuates performance, advancing us to another level. While to a certain extent the left or right hemispheres of the brain can, and do, function independently of one another, they work best when integrated and grounded by the central nervous system. When we meditate we are aligning and harmonizing our electrical system. But we must be grounded!

Another crucial meditative ingredient is vocalization. In vocalizing a mantra it is the resulting resonant vibration that, with patience and practice, can align and harmonize our mind and body. Vibration is essential to enlightenment. Enlightenment occurs gradually through meditation. It is attained through grounded vibration, a deep resonance, that produces equilibrium: unity, peace, and harmony of body, mind, and spirit with love, relief, and truth as a way of life. What "God"—whoever he might be—wants is in our hearts and minds: the Red and White Stones. God wants us to love him, love ourselves, and love others. Charity is love in action, selfless service on behalf of others without expectation of recognition or benefit. "God" wants us to *live* by example, to stimulate awareness of God's omnipresence, omnipotence, and omniscience; God wants us to educate, inspire, and motivate others to be the best that they can be, to live in harmony with nature and one another without domination as an egalitarian society envisioned by Dee and Bacon. Once the light is experienced we are not and cannot be as we once were. Enlightenment is traveling that broad level of time to an undiscovered country, to Arcadia, from whose bourn no person returns. You are forever changed!

Charles was an enlightened soul. He was a thoughtful, quiet, humble man who had a positive impact on the lives of many. It wasn't until he died that I became aware of just how many lives Charles had touched. Hundreds of people turned out for his memorial service. Friends queued outside the church in the cold to say their goodbyes to him. His wife, family, and friends—we all have our unique stories to tell of Charles's kindness and good deeds. He was an influential positive force in our lives. He was a dear friend. It was an honor and privilege to have known him. But Charles hadn't always been kind or good. He had a turbulent past too. What is important is that he was able to change. With a fire in his belly Charles transmuted his heart and mind from those of a base metal, distilling his thoughts and deeds. In the end his character was as pure and hard as diamond. He embodied the Philosophers' Stone.

When Charles died he was released from his terrestrial bonds. His corporeal time had expired, and we all celebrated the life that had touched our lives. His legacy is one of peace and friendship, doing good unto all. While Charles's passing was seemingly tragic and untimely, it was necessary. His life had created a pocket of order in a chaotic world. His death was necessary so that we who knew him might be reborn, grow, and advance, becoming more than we once were. Charles lives on in the lives of those he touched. Remember, life is everlasting.

Charles's gift to me was a wealth of knowledge about life, about death; about how everything is part of the ALL and that the ALL is part of everything—about oneness. During my time with Charles he taught me much about the mountain. "This mountain, she is old, and she is sacred. She has a strong spirit," he said. "She will test your spirit when you come here alone. You must show her respect. If you are strong of spirit and respect her, maybe she will share her secrets."

*Figure 11.1. Charles in the Channels, an omphalos and womb of the Earth.*

Upon his death I inherited Charles's spirit and that of teachers who came before him in a form of resurrection. Like a serpent shedding its skin, I was renewed, and I experienced a beginning without end much as an ouroboros, as Ophiuchus. In spring, after the snowmelt, we spread Charles's ashes on the mountain, returning him whence he came. Afterward, with red and white stripes painted on my cheeks to show that I lived, died, and was resurrected, I ventured on the mountain alone. The mountain, she tested me three more times: first with a black coyote, second with a bobcat, and third with a bear. Each time I could have easily been maimed or killed. But I survived. I survived and returned to sing songs of my adventure. Charles was right, you must be strong and respectful on the mountain. You see, Charles was a raven. He was Hermes, the messenger of the gods who traveled between the three worlds as a spiritual magician, healer, and teacher. He was a guardian of the mountain and keeper of her secrets. He too was reborn that spring. As for me, I became something else. I am Xas'i, the little snake. I have brought you by a way that you knew not, led you along paths that you did not know, made darkness light before you, and crooked things straight (Isaiah 42:16). I have performed my duty as Principal Sojourner in Royal Arch Masonry and provided sustenance such as I have as the Hermit encountered along your path to become a Knight Templar. As with Percival, I have shown you the Grail.

There is a flower growing high up on a mountain. Go to this mountain. Find this flower. Come back, sing your song, and share tales of your adventure! *Gochine* (blessings) my friend!

# THE HERMIT'S LANTERN

Knowledge comes to each of us from many places and in many ways. When we have eyes to see, ears to hear, and a heart to recognize and appreciate it for what it is, when we are duly and truly prepared to receive it, knowledge comes. In this book we've likened the path to that of the three degrees of Masonry using the phrase Bell, Book, and Candle. The initiate answers the bell—the call—in the first degree. In the second degree, he studies the book—many books. In the third degree, there is illumination—the light of the candle. Comprehending the three elements of this phrase is important for any initiate seeking spiritual illumination and an understanding of the Philosophers' Stone. It's a simple, beautiful analogy!

Our hearts and minds are the essence of the Philosophers' Stone. The irony is that bell, book, and candle were used by the Vatican in a ceremony to excommunicate heretics, freethinkers who chose to question and not blindly place absolute faith in Church doctrine, freethinkers who chose to seek and worship God in their own way. After all, worshipping God is a personal matter. How we worship God is not subject to the dictates of others. What God wants is what is in our hearts and minds. And we must not forget charity, which is love in action, setting aside our ego to help others without the expectation of reward or acknowledgment, doing what we know in our hearts and minds to be right. Living by example and being the best that we can be in God's eyes and the eyes of our fellow humans, we create awareness, educate, inspire, and motivate others to do the same. We become a source of peace, unity, and harmony.

Transcendence, the path of the Philosophers' Stone, the path of enlightenment, is painful and difficult, as are life and death, birth and re-birth. We are but fools traveling this path, a path where we are beset by ruffians all along the way. The path is a process in which we distill ourselves, endeavoring to become as small and pure as a grain of salt, a perfect ashlar, in our quest for knowledge and truth, the Grail.

Look up! Look up and see the light of the Hermit's lantern illuminating your way. Look up! Look up and see Charles on the mountaintop!

# NOTES

## INTRODUCTION.
## MY CURIOSITY FOR TRUTH

1. Mike Kelley (creator), "Perception," *Revenge* (TV show), season 1 episode 14 (Los Angeles, Calif., and Southampton, N.Y.: The Page Front Company/ Mike Kelley Productions, 2011–2015).

## CHAPTER 1.
## THE ORDER OF OPHIUCHUS

1. Greek Travel Tellers, "Mysteries of Ancient Greece You Didn't Know About."
2. Press, *Development of the Idea of History in Antiquity.*

## CHAPTER 3.
## THE KINGDOM OF HEAVEN

1. Roob, *The Hermetic Museum,* 429.
2. Chapin, *Living Words,* 70.
3. Albert Schweitzer, BrainyQuote.com, Xplore Inc.
4. Ridley Scott (director), *Kingdom of Heaven* (United States: Scott Free Productions, 2005).
5. Mike Kelley (creator), "Perception," *Revenge* (TV show), season 1 episode 14.
6. The first three lines of this paragraph come from Rupert Wainwright's film *Stigmata* (Los Angeles: Metro-Goldwyn-Mayer, 1999). They combine the thought of the Gospel of St. Thomas sayings 3a and 77b.

166

## CHAPTER 4. THE PHILOSOPHERS' STONE

1. Feynman, *The Meaning of It All,* 15.
2. Maier, *Atalanta Fugiens,* emblem and discourse XXI.

## CHAPTER 5. AN OBLONG SQUARE

1. Maier, *Atalanta Fugiens,* discourse XXXIX.
2. Maier, *Atalanta Fugiens,* discourse XXXIX.

## CHAPTER 6. ELEMENTS OF THE STONE

1. Hogan, *The Alchemical Keys to Masonic Ritual,* 19.
2. Flammel, *Alchemical Hieroglyphics,* 72.
3. Fryar, *Aureus: The Golden Tractate of Hermes Trismegistus,* 1 and 2.
4. Atwood, *A Suggestive Inquiry into the Hermetic Mystery.*
5. Eckhardt, *Secret Symbols of the Rosicrucians,* 16.
6. Richards, *Invisibility: Mastering the Art of Vanishing,* 36.
7. Maier, *Atalanta Fugiens,* discourse XXXIX.
8. Jungwirth, "How Many Waters Are Necessary to Dissolve a Rock Salt Molecule?" 145–48.
9. Cloe, "The Actions of Sodium in the Human Body."
10. Shastri, *The Linga-Purana.*

## CHAPTER 7. LIFE AND DEATH

1. Three Initiates, *The Kybalion.*
2. Lumen Learning website, "The Laws of Thermodynamics."
3. Mayo Clinic, *Pregnancy Week by Week.*
4. U.S. Geological Survey, "The Water in You: Water and the Human Body."

## CHAPTER 8. THE STAIRWAY TO HEAVEN

1. Savige, "Electrical Design in the Human Body."
2. All about Circuits, "Voltage and Current," chapter 1, "Basic Concepts of Electricity."
3. Taylor, "Voltage, Current, Resistance, and Ohm's Law.

4. Northwestern University Mechatronics, "Resistors (Ohm's Law), Capacitors, and Inductors."

5. Elert, "Simple Harmonic Generator."

6. Electronics Tutorials, "Electrical Waveforms. Waveform Generators."

7. The Free Dictionary online, s.v. "Positional Servomechanism."

8. The Stroke Network, "Thalamus."

9. Sargis, "An Overview of the Pineal Gland."

10. Sargis, "An Overview of the Pituitary Gland."

## CHAPTER 9. REGENERATION

1. Tolle, *A New Earth*.

# BIBLIOGRAPHY

All about Circuits. "Voltage and Current," chapter 1, "Basic Concepts of Electricity." AllaboutCircuits website. Accessed June 14, 2018.

Atwood, Mary Anne. *A Suggestive Inquiry into the Hermetic Mystery with a Dissertation on the More Celebrated of the Alchemical Philosophers being an Attempt Towards the Recovery of the Ancient Experiment of Nature.* Belfast: William Tait, 1918.

Chapin, Edwin Hubbell. *Living Words.* Boston: N.E. Universalist Publishing House, 1866.

Cloe, Adam. "The Actions of Sodium in the Human Body." *Healthy Eating,* SFGate website. Accessed June 6, 2018.

Eckhardt, J. D. A. *Secret Symbols of the Rosicrucians of the 16th & 17th Centuries.* Altona, 1785.

Egan, James Alan. *John Dee's America: The Idea of America Came from the Mind of John Dee, and Rhode Island's First Governor, Benedict Arnold, Helped Make It a Reality.* Newport, RI: Cosmopolite Press, 2015.

———. *The Newport Tower Is John Dee's 1583 New World Church of the Holy Sepulcher.* Newport, RI: Cosmopolite Press, 2012.

Electronics Tutorials. "Electrical Waveforms. Waveform Generators." ElectronicsTutorials website. Accessed June 14, 2018.

Elert, Glenn. "Simple Harmonic Generator." *The Physics Hypertextbook* website.

Feynman, Richard P. *The Meaning of It All: Thoughts of a Citizen-Scientist.* New York: Basic Books, 2005.

Flammel, Nicholas. *Alchemical Hieroglyphics.* Berkeley Heights, NJ: Heptangle Books, 1980.

Fryar, Robert H. *Aureus: The Golden Tractate of Hermes Trismegistus, concerning the Physical Secret of the Philosopher's Stone, in Seven Sections.* Bath, 1886.

Greek Travel Tellers. "Mysteries of Ancient Greece You Didn't Know About." GreekTravelTellers website, January 25, 2020.

Hogan, Timothy. *The Alchemical Keys to Masonic Ritual*. Lulu.com, 2007.

Jungwirth, Pavel. "How Many Waters Are Necessary to Dissolve a Rock Salt Molecule?" *Journal of Physical Chemistry* 104, no. 1 (December 11, 1999):145–48.

Lepee, Edward. "Biographical Tableau." *Freemasons' Quarterly Magazine*, vol. 2. G. Routledge & Co., London. 1851.

Lumen Learning, "The Laws of Thermodynamics." Lumen Learning website. Accessed June 7, 2018.

Maier, Michael. *Atalanta Fugiens*. Illustrated by Matthias Merian, printed by Hieronymous Galler, published by Johann Theodor de Bry. Oppenheim, 1617. Transcriptions by Hereward Tilton and Peter Branwin available on Adam Maclean's Alchemy website.

Mayo Clinic Staff. "Pregnancy Week by Week." Healthy Lifestyle, Mayo Clinic website. Accessed June 14, 2018.

Northwestern University Mechatronics. "Resistors (Ohm's Law), Capacitors, and Inductors." Accessed June 14, 2018.

Pike, Albert, and Arturo De Hoyos. *Albert Pike's Morals and Dogma of the Ancient and Accepted Scottish Rite of Freemasonry, Annotated Edition*. Washington, D.C.: The Supreme Council 33° Southern Jurisdiction, U.S.A., 2011.

Press, Gerald A. *Development of the Idea of History in Antiquity*. Montreal, Canada, and Kingston, New York: McGill-Queen's University Press, (1982) 2003.

Richards, Steve. *Invisibility: Mastering the Art of Vanishing*. San Francisco: Weiser Books, 2013.

Roob, Alexander. *The Hermetic Museum: Alchemy and Mysticism*. Köln: Taschen GmbH, 2015.

Sargis, Robert M. "An Overview of the Pineal Gland: Maintaining Circadian Rhythm." Endocrineweb, June 20, 2014.

———. "An Overview of the Pituitary Gland: The Endocrine System's Master Gland." Endocrineweb, April 10, 2018.

Savige, Craig. "Electrical Design in the Human Body." Answers in Genesis website, December 1, 1999. Originally published in *Creation* 22, no. 1 (December 1999): 43–45.

Shastri, J. L. *The Linga-Purana*. Delhi: Montilal Banarsidass, 1951. Available on Internet Archive.

The Stroke Network. "Thalamus." Stroke Education, The Stroke Network website. Accessed June 14, 2018.

Taylor, C. "Voltage, Current, Resistance, and Ohm's Law." Tutorials, Sparkfun website.

Three Initiates. *The Kybalion*. Northamptonshire, UK: White Crane, 2011.

Tolle, Eckhart. *A New Earth: Awakening to Your Life's Purpose*. 10th ed. New York: Penguin, 2016.

U. S. Geological Survey. "The Water in You: Water and the Human Body." U.S.G.S. website (May 22, 2019). Accessed December 21, 2022.

# INDEX